THE KEMET FILES

THE KEMET FILES

An Inquiry
Concerning Racism,
Monotheism and Early Civilization

by
Robert J Bridges

Element Press
California

THE KEMET FILES

Element Press
California

Copyright © 2021 by Robert Joseph Bridges
Interior Illustrations by the Author

All rights reserved.
No part of this book may be reproduced in any form or by any means electronic, photocopying, recording, or otherwise, without permission in writing from the publisher, except by a reviewer who may quote brief passages in a review.

Second edition
ISBN: 978-0-9858722-4-3
Printed in the
United States
of America

THE KEMET FILES

**For the
people of the
African Diaspora**

Contents

Page

1 Introduction

10 Oyinbo

19 First Humans

24 First Monotheism

30 Aten-Monotheism

49 Deception

70 African Monotheism * White Judaism

83 First Civilization

95 First Art and Science

120 Tale of Two Continents

132 On Race and Status

153 African Influence in America

165 African Renaissance

Appendices

Page:

173 (A) Inventors

182 (B) Symbols of Wisdom

186 (C) Bantu in America

191 Notes

195 Bibliography

Introduction

The African origin of civilization is written within these pages of African history. Of course, factual African history is important for many reasons. Especially because history helps to dispel dangerous myths, ideas, and falsehoods such as the notion of white supremacy. And the ideology of racism, that falsely suggests an innate, inherent superiority of whites over the innate, inherent inferiority of people of African descent. When properly understood, the effects of racism have to do with power—the relative power between whites and people of African descent. The disparity in relative power between these two groups in America is plain to see through social indicators such as income, wealth, education, and criminal justice statistics among others. These statistics illustrate that despite any contrary argument, racism and white supremacy is current and prevalent in the United States today.

Obviously, when racism permeates the judicial, legislative, and executive branches of government and society in general, it likely influences policy, legislation and voting rights. Because with systemic racism, policies and laws are purposely put into place to intentionally impeded the progress of the people of African descent.

Racism will persist until its effects are undone. When a fire consumes a house for example, the effect of the fire remains until a renovation takes place. In the same way, institutional racism and all its ill effects, requires transformation from the ground up. This kind of transformation took place in German society where in addition to reparations, there was a sincere attempt to reconcile the actions of its sordid past. For example, Germany provided reparations and passed legislation making it a crime to deny the holocaust or to display a swastika.

In America, there has been a reluctant passing of civil rights legislation, but no truth, no reconciliation, and no factual African history acknowledged or taught to break the cycle of white supremacy. To expect reparations from a white supremacist society is nonsensical. Nazi Germany would have never given reparations to Jews. That happened only after Germany cured itself from white supremacy. In fact, civil rights legislation had more to do with the Russian cold war than any altruism on the part of the US towards African descendants. Racism in the US, left little room to criticize the lack of freedom in communist Russia;

thus, Russia and the world were watching and waiting for America to clean up its own back yard. What was at stake was America's cold war influence over third world nations versus communist Russia's. Hence, civil rights legislation reluctantly passed. But without truth and reconciliation; racism will continue to endure. Modern day police abuse and murders of unarmed Black men is symbolic of America's enduring racism; and the confederate flag, still legal, and flying, symbolizes an enduring racism in the US.

There has been progressive government intervention and reconciliation regarding the public image and treatment of white Jews in America, mainly due to the influence of right-wing neo-conservatives led by Ronald Reagan. Reconciliation for African descent people in America could be similar. Police reform is imperative. Racist cops are byproducts of the white supremacy system in which they were bred. And social media such as Yahoo Comments, and Quora, serving as virtual incubators of hate, there are more racist cops in the pipeline.

We must leverage our $1.84 trillion buying power to affect change and fight racism in the US and around the world. Because we know politicians are non-responsive to the needs of the African descent community, but they do listen to CEOs. United African American consumers could leverage buying power to effect change. In fact, this could be the new methodology to redress our grievances; because the old way through the political process has been an exercise in futility. This is due above all to the fact that politicians today are financed and controlled by corporations.

To implication that America is not racist today without having had any attempt what so ever to cure itself from racism through police reform legislation, education, media campaigns, truth and reconciliation, reparations, or other means, is nonsensical. Racism and the legacy of racism is present today in American society and like any disease it will remain until a cure is provided. It is pervasive and contagious. To deny that America is a racist society is the same as saying the earth does not rotate on its axis; because it is so pervasive and constant that we cannot see or feel it rotating. Racism and white supremacy in the US is as pervasive as the rotation of the earth. And such a constant within the fabric of American society that for some, it conveniently appears to not exist. And sadly, it refuses to cure itself.

Therefore, without a cooperative consumer effort to counter its ill effects, racism as an ideology will persist. Yet, as our journey through history unfolds, it will become clear that racism is a false ideology. Because all humans are over 99.9% identical, genetically. In other words, the concept of race has no scientific basis and is simply a false notion. Yet, the social construct of racism is very real. It subjugates people of African descent to the lower-class levels of society; and policies and laws are enacted to make sure most of them remain there.

A full disclosure of Africa's hidden history chronicling its origin of civilization combined with the unification of African consumers, could render racism ineffective, because history reveals that Africans created the first civilization, not whites. Human civilization originated through African discoveries and inventions such as astronomy, geometry, mathematics, architecture, philosophy, engineering, medicine, surgery, writing, grammar, an alphabet, sculpture and art. They also wrote the first holy books and built the first temples to worship and practice spirituality, religion and the first monotheism. Established the first college devoted to higher learning in Egypt, at Annu, which is the biblical ON; and the first University at Timbuktu in West Africa and more. The African civilizing discoveries and inventions negate the false and ridiculous notion of white supremacy. There has been a concerted effort to malign African descent people and marginalize their historical contributions through lies and omission.

Ancient Egyptians and Nubians were ethnic African people meaning Black people. So the process of marginalizing, denying and omitting the African contribution is to deny that Egyptians and Nubians were Black people. This is because ancient Egyptians and Nubians originated the arts and sciences above, and thus, originated the first civilizations known to man. And the African origination of civilization refutes the ridiculous notion of white supremacy.

Sadly, most Egyptologists were racists and went to great lengths to deny what the Greek historian Herodotus witnessed about the ancient Egyptians with his own eyes; "Their skin was black and their hair was wooly." Instead, they would claim that black skinned Egyptians were not African, and even more laughable, that Nubians were white people with black skin. This is the extent to which the African contribution has been hidden or omitted from the world, to give credence to the false notion of white supremacy. Most Egyptologists could not tolerate history without revision, particularly when it came to African achievement; mainly due to a cognitive dissonance. Cognitive dissonance makes it difficult for one to accept facts that go against their core belief system; for example, white supremacy. A study of mummy DNA for example, should include mummies from the Old Kingdom or Middle Kingdom; not just mummies from later foreign invaders who arrived well after the arts and sciences were established by the Ancient Egyptians. To extrapolate from that sample the idea that the Ancient Egyptians came not from the African interior but from outside Africa, again, protects their core belief system of white supremacy; further enabling a cognitive dissonance of all other facts such as the time needed to develop the arts and sciences. For example, modern humans evolved in Africa 300,000 years ago. And the Nabta Playa astronomers began to track the stars circa 12,000BC. Then through mutation (SLC24A5), came the first modern human beings with white skin 10,000BC. This demonstrates a lack of sufficient time for the white skin migration out of Africa, separation, and later mixing with Africans to produce the human variety of skin color we see today. How could they in that short amount of time on earth, build the Ancient Egyptian and Nubian civilizations? The first astronomical observatory was built by Africans in Nabta Playa in 6,000BC. The first calendar was invented in Egypt in 4,236BC. Since it takes 7,000 years to accumulated enough astronomical data to invent stellar and lunar calendars, it would have been impossible for whites to produce the Egyptian calendar in 4,236BC as they were still nomadic cave dwellers in Europe.

Monotheism is also a part of history and the first monotheism was invented in Africa. Christianity is the daughter of that monotheistic religion invented in Africa. Some historians like Egyptologists, also experienced cognitive dissonance regarding various historical facts.

For example, Flavius Josephus who wrote the so-called history of the Jews confused the Hyksos as the people of the Exodus; and consequently, claimed Mesopotamia as the birthplace of the biblical Hebrew. This mistake influenced his writing on Jewish history. The Hyksos expulsion out of Egypt by the Pharaoh Ahmose, however, occurred in 1550 BC; the biblical exodus took place circa 1350 BC. These are two distinct events in Egyptian history. In fact, the story of the biblical exodus occurs during the time of the Pharaoh Akhenaten's monotheistic revolution in Egypt. In addition, the events in the life of the biblical Moses represent that of the Egyptian Pharaoh, Akhenaten, the first monotheist. Obviously, Josephus sought to distance the biblical Exodus from the monotheistic revolution that took place in Egypt under the Pharaoh Akhenaten. Yet, that monotheistic revolution occurred at the same time as the biblical Exodus; and the ten commandments, which were written on papyrus in hieroglyphs and kept today inside the Vatican were taken from the 42 Egyptian Negative Confessions. Also, in Palestine/Israel, pottery was found to be decorated in hieroglyphs. Finally, the first seat of the Christian Church was in Africa, not Italy. The Romans, with no religious affinity, transferred the seat of the church to Rome, which enabled them to govern the people more efficiently. While European missionaries converted native people around the globe for the purpose of subjugation and for looting the land and wealth. In the context of that colonialism and African history, a whitewashed Christianity reinforces white supremacy. There has been a whitewashing of what initially was an offshoot of African religion that developed from the uniquely African experiences of life and death, and from the African concept of the resurrection and salvation of the spiritual soul that eventually refined into African religion and monotheism.

In regards to white supremacy, knowledge of the

African origin of civilization dispels it. Therefore, African history is necessary for whites in America and throughout the world if they want to cure themselves from white supremacy, which is a mental disorder. And for African descendants, true African history is necessary to spark the cultural renaissance.

Now let us explore our African history back to the birth of humanity, before any concept of religion or *race*. Time and settlement and a level of spiritual, ethical, and moral sophistication was needed to develop a religion in general; but the African ideological leap to monotheism was due to a series of political events, which we will cover later. Race? There was no concept of race because the original humans were ethnic Africans with color in their skins and color producing melanin in their genetic makeup. In the beginning, there were no white people. The question as to how and when they arrived will be revealed as we uncover our hidden African history.

1

Oyinbo

With respect to matrilineal lineage, the most recent common ancestor of all living humans is known as the Mitochondrial Eve. Her DNA code, the complete instructions for making a human, passed down through the generations, and is present today in all humans. This means that the Mitochondrial Eve, born in Africa, is the mother of all humanity.

A genetic mutation, on occasion will deviate from that original DNA information. Mutations are a part of natural evolution, and can be advantageous to a species, enabling them to adapt more successfully to their environment. Yet, mutations can be a disadvantage, as well, by altering one's ability to adapt suitably to the environment, thus increasing the likelihood of succumbing to sickness or death. Over time however, such a mutation, if recessive, will self-correct through natural selection and purge itself out of the gene pool.

This brings us to an essential part of our hidden African history, which focuses on the small difference in the genetic make-up between humans. A major part of that minute difference is the effect of a gene mutation, which occurred in humans thousands of years ago. That gene mutation, although recessive, somehow bucked the trend of natural selection, and survived to modern day. Yet, how does a recessive gene mutation survive the natural selection powers of a more populous, dominant gene? The answer to this question will uncover the genesis of *race*.

Scientist at Penn state University has discovered perhaps the most important gene mutation in the history of humanity–the skin-whitening mutation. The mutated skin-whitening gene, SLC24A5, is recessive and deprives whites of the ability to produce color. And because gene mutations occur infrequently, the SLC24A5 gene carriers today, represent a minority of the world population.

> The newly found mutation involves a change of just one letter of DNA code out of the 3.1 billion letters in the human genome -- the complete instructions for making a human being.

The article continues:

> Scientists said yesterday that they have discovered a tiny genetic mutation that largely explains the first appearance of white skin in human beings tens of thousands of years ago, a finding that helps solve one of biology's most enduring mysteries and illuminates one of humanity's greatest sources of strife.
>
> The work suggests that the skin-whitening mutation occurred by chance in a single individual after the first human exodus from Africa, when all people were brown-skinned. That person's offspring apparently thrived as humans moved northward into what is now Europe, helping to give rise to the lightest of the world's races.[1]

The author of the article opines that the study suggests that the skin whitening mutation gene, SLC24A5, occurred in a single individual after the migration out of Africa thousands of years ago when all people had skin color. Whether it is possible, however, for a person with a genetic recessive skin-whitening mutation, to procreate with melanin producing African people around her and produce white offspring, is the question. Nature, it seems, would have corrected such a defect each time she bred with a dominant melanin producing individual. This is natural selection at work, and it occurs because a recessive mutated gene such as the SLC24A5 gene would leave the carrier vulnerable in their environment, necessitating a correction.

In this case, melanin produces color to protect the skin from the sun's deadly radiation. Because without the ability to produce color, white skin is susceptible to sun burning and deadly skin cancers; especially in the sweltering heat of Africa. Natural selection would normally purge such genes from the genome, especially in a single white individual surrounded by dominant melanin producing gene carriers, but why not in this case.

Since the skin whitening gene is recessive, in order for the gene to past down to the next generation, the recessive gene carrier would have to breed with another recessive mutated gene carrier. In other words, there had to have been a cluster of SLC24A5 gene carriers, living and breeding amongst each other, prior to the migration to Europe.

Once their numbers became sufficient, and segregated away from the dominant melanin producing gene carriers, they would buck the trend of natural selection and produce more and more white offspring. If a white skinned mutated gene carrier procreates with a melanin producing gene carrier, however, the recessive mutated gene washes out because the melanin producing gene is dominant. Therefore, the suggestion that a single individual with a recessive skin whitening mutation could produce white offspring in the midst of melanin producing people of color is implausible.

Normally, if a gene mutation occurs randomly in a single individual, as is the case with the SLC24A5 gene, a correction of the recessive gene mutation takes place when the carrier procreates with dominant gene carriers. Therefore, something peculiar in nature had to occur, in order for the recessive skin-whitening gene to buck the trend of natural selection and flourish. We see today that if say, a woman form Germany procreates with an African man, the offspring would be a person of color, able to produce melanin. This same result would take place today or circa 10,000 BC because the African possesses the dominant color producing gene. And if this pattern of mating between an African man and a German woman were to repeat among an entire German population, the resulting offspring would have color–thus Natural Selection at work.

Sexual selection is an evolutionary theory posed by Charles Darwin, perhaps to explain the anomaly of why, in a case such as this, the not-so-fittest survived. Yet, if people were sexually attracted to an individual because of their difference, such as skin color, it would not explain how a single white individual could be the progenitor of an entire white population, given the dominant nature of the melanin/color producing individuals with whom she procreates. The opposite of this mythical *sexual selection* would be something more practical, especially regarding the skin-whitening mutation.

A cluster of skin-whitening gene carriers, congregated amongst one another to breed. This is the only exclamation as to why the recessive skin-whitening gene fails to select naturally, or remove itself, out of the dominant melanin producing population. How and why did this phenomenon occur?

Studies have shown that the occurrence of skin whitening gene mutations in Africa is 1 in 10,000. This suggests that a significant population cluster of skin whitening mutations occurred in Africa prior to the migration out.

Let us start our journey in Africa tens of thousands of years ago. A newborn boy we will call Oyinbo, was afflicted with the skin-whitening gene mutation SLC24A5. He was born in the middle of the night and slept next to his mother. The following morning, there was panic and fear throughout the camp because of the baby's white skin. The father rejects the baby, but the mother, although consumed by apprehension and fear; nurtured the baby. She hoped that one day the baby's skin would darken like all the other children in the camp. But the other children feared to go near him since none of them had ever laid eyes on a human with white skin. Try as he may, the children and adults in the camp would not allow Oyinbo near them. As he got older, even his mother grew tired of waiting for his skin to darken and would care for him no longer. Oyinbo, shunned and ostracized by the group, sets out alone.

He leaves the camp and wonders about in the wilderness. Along the way, he is pleased to discover others with the same skin-whitening mutation, ostracized from their respective camps, as he was, surviving in the wilderness. They grouped together and depended on one another for survival as they hunted and gathered food. Soon, they would encounter even more white skinned individuals, shunned and ostracized from their respective groups. Because they shared the recessive skin-whitening gene mutation, they bred white offspring.

Due to the ancient African fear of white skin, coupled with the ostracism and isolation of the recessive skin-whitening gene carriers, natural selection, in this case, did not take place. The ostracized group of whites mated with each other and grew their population. However, although the recessive gene survived, it was inadequate protection from the intense sunlight inside Africa; therefore, Oyinbo and his white skinned group would seek a climate more conducive to their survival.

Migration

About 50,000 years ago, the first humans migrated out of Africa. Among the pre historic

Africans who migrated into Europe were the Grimaldi. Thousands of years later, the white SLC24A5 gene type would also migrate out of Africa as a group, north into Europe.

There, they found refuge, and would eventually outnumber the Grimaldi people, why? The colder region of Europe was a more suitable environment for the SLC24A5 gene carriers. Not only because their white skin was no longer vulnerable to the intense African sunlight; but because white skin, more efficiently than skin of color, was able to absorb important levels of vitamin D, from the less intense European sunlight.

Interestingly, Neanderthal man, first discovered in western Germany, also had white skin. However, the Neanderthal's white skin was the result of a suitable adaptation to the cold environment of Europe. Therefore, while nature selects the paleness of the Neanderthal, while the paleness of the modern white human results from mutation. Although according to the research published in *Science* Magazine 7 May 2010, by the Max-Planck Institute of Evolutionary Anthropology of Germany, Neanderthal DNA does indeed exist within the genome of all modern Europeans. Apparently, interbreeding took place between humans and Neanderthals in Europe, after the migration out of Africa.

Over the next tens of thousands of years, the SLC24A5 group became isolated in Europe, and adapted to their environment, away from the rest of humanity.

Later, however, a mix or Semite type appeared because of the interbreeding over time between the SLC24A5 gene types and Africans who lived in Asia and perhaps parts of Europe. This is evident by simple deduction. The original people with melanin produced dark skin were one color until a second type arrived (SLC24A5) due to mutation. The mixture between them produces skin color, but skin color that lay somewhere in between, such as the Semite type. Today, the SLC24A5 types represent perhaps only ten percent of the world's population. Keep in mind that racism and colonialism perpetuated upon the subjected people a white European standard of beauty. This has caused indigenous peoples to reject their own natural beauty and features. Particularly their beautiful skin color, which is natural and designed to protect them from the sun's deadly radiation. Ironically, most whites desire to have at least some color in their skin; hence the reason for the obsessive sun tanning especially when living in close proximity to people of color. Conversely, many formerly colonized non-African people desire to be white for reasons mentioned above and reject the original melanin producing people of African descent from whom all the world's people derived.

2

First Humans

Meanwhile most original humans remained and settled in Africa near water systems, like the seasonal Nabta Playa, Nile River and the Great Lakes, eventually spreading throughout the continent of Africa. Their task was to master the environment and begin to build the first human civilization.

The catalyst that drove the blossoming civilization was the Nile River itself. The African settlers observed and closely measured over time, the rising and falling crest of the river, which became an important source of irrigation for agricultural crops and domesticated animals. Each year at the beginning of summer solstice, the river would rise for one hundred straight days— after which it would recede. This effect was due to the melting snows in the north and increasing summer temperatures. Overtime, they recognized a correlation between the position of the stars in the night sky and the beginning of the annual summer solstice, which enabled them to anticipate the annual flooding and recession of the river.

Even before the settlement of the Nile Valley, Africans observed and recorded the movement of the stars for thousands of years, beginning in an area of the Nubian Desert known as Nabta Playa.

In Nabta Playa, scientists discovered a stone Calendar Circle and observatory that was in use by Africans between 10,000 BC and 6,000 BC. Because of this practice of astronomy at Nabta Playa, Africans would eventually invent the lunar calendar in the year 4236 BC. The invention of the lunar calendar, which consists of a 365 day and 12-month year with a correction every fourth year, is the result of thousands of years of data collection and observation by the African astronomers. These African astronomers were the progeny of the first and original modern humans, who evolved in Africa 200,000 years ago. To put this in perspective, the SLC24A5 mutated type only made their first appearance in the world in circa 10,000 BC.

Astronomy enabled people of the Nile Valley, to utilize the Nile for irrigation purposes, and to predict the inundation of the river. This led to the invention and refining of agricultural technique and the development of geometry as a means to measure and layout fields for crop growing; and to properly assess property boundaries after the flooding of the Nile. The practice of measuring the earth gave rise to architectural mathematics and the construction of buildings, temples and monuments. Settlement also led to the development of spirituality and religion.

While nomadic people burned their dead, the settled Africans near the Nile buried their dead; since there was a belief in the resurrection of the spirit, burial was simply preparation for the afterlife. The tombs that the Pharaohs built for themselves in preparation for the afterlife became more elaborate over time. The Great Pyramids are living monuments attesting to this fact. Nubians and Egyptians developed their religious tradition from this context. And led to the authorship of spiritual books that contained hundreds of moralistic principles about life and creation, as well as instructions on preparation for an afterlife. Perhaps the most famous of those writings is the *Book of the Dead*, the first holy book ever written, dating to 4000 BC.

Because of their belief in an afterlife, their spiritual writings and funerary ritual began to reflect this over time. Upon a person's death for example, a judge weighed an individual's heart (conscience) to assure that it equaled the weight of a feather before proceeding to the afterlife.

Their sacred writings include stories relating to deities such as the trinity of Isis, Osiris, and Horus.

There is a recognition of Isis and the baby Horus as the Madonna and child throughout Europe— particularly Eastern Europe, where worship of the Black Madonna continues today.

This worship of Isis, the Black Madonna, by Europeans should be of no surprise when one considers the Greeks and Romans, who borrowed many of the Nubian and Egyptian gods and renamed them in their own respective language. Indeed, Christianity itself borrowed much from Nubian and Egyptian religion; including a holy trinity and the concept of spiritual salvation and resurrection.

Religion is among the many discoveries that Greece and Rome borrowed from Africa's initial development of man's first civilization. The calendar, mathematics, geometry, astronomy, writing, art, sculptor, architecture, philosophy, engineering, medicine, and surgery are among the others. Unfortunately, these great discoveries and knowledge has dispersed to the world not by the Africans who originated them, but by the Greeks and Romans who copied them.

Socrates, Aristotle, and Pythagoras all studied their philosophy and science in Egypt, while Greece and Rome dispersed this African knowledge into Europe by way of war and trade; hence are given credit for having developed it. Further, the discoveries and inventions of the renaissance period in Europe could not have come about without the scientific, mathematical, and architectural knowledge from Africa. This knowledge, which was lost in Europe after the fall of Rome, was reintroduced into Europe by the hidden Greek and Roman manuscripts of African knowledge and by the African Moors who were guardians of the African knowledge, particularly mathematical theory. Thus, Africa, once again would propel Europe out of the ignorance of the Dark Ages, into the renaissance.

Obviously, knowledge, if unimpeded will spread quickly. For example, at some point in time, many nations of the world will be able to produce nuclear weaponry, despite the attempt to keep the technology proprietary or secret. This type of knowledge when fully expanded can influence human society greatly. Other ideas such as *race* or religion can influence humanity greatly as well. The uncovering of the genesis or conception of both race and religion are essential in understanding the motivation behind racism.

3

First Monotheism

Monotheism, the religious ideology first invented by Africans, has fully dispersed around the world, and has had a tremendous impact upon human behavior. While monotheism was a major ideological leap, it was also a rather practical transformation. Africans in Egypt and Nubia had an established tradition of unifying a series of lesser deities under one greater deity. Ra, for example, was a chief deity over the lesser ones of Egypt. Over time, newer deities would possibly usurp the powers and significance of much older ones, such as Ra, to some degree, if not altogether and become a chief deity. The transition to monotheism began with this idea of the one chief deity, but a catalyst was necessary to propel such a transition forward.

The catalyst that caused this radical yet practical transformation from polytheism to monotheism began to seed in Egypt since the very first dynasty. The unity of Upper and Lower Egypt was an essential political undertaking. The first Pharaoh Narmer succeeded in doing just that and established a unified Egypt's first dynasty. In an act of political expediency, aimed to strengthen the new union, Narmer combined both the red and white crowns of Upper and Lower Egypt, and made it into one. The new crown of the united Egypt also symbolized the unity of the chief and important gods of Upper and Lower Egypt—Amen and Ra; hence, appeasing the populations of both territories and moving an ideological step forward toward the worship of one deity—monotheism.

In the 15th dynasty, Egypt fell under the occupation of Hyksos shepherds in predominately Lower Egypt. After one hundred years of occupation, the Pharaoh Ahmose defeated them in battle. Ahmose freed Lower Egypt from the grips of the invaders and united it with Upper Egypt once again and made Thebes in Upper Egypt its capitol. Since Amen was the chief deity of Thebes, he became exceedingly more powerful over Ra, after the victory. Ahmose, and each succeeding Pharaoh in turn (excepting Thutmose IV, Amenhotep III and Akhenaton) showered the priests of Thebes with wealth and power.

A succession of pharaohs loyal to Amen, reigned over a united Egypt after Ahmose's defeat of the

Hyksos. As a result, over time, Amen of Thebes became ever more exalted as a deity and more powerful than all of the deities that existed before him which included Ra.

However, when Thutmose IV came to power, he began to favor Ra, the stellar deity, and his successor Amenhotep III, would do the same. The Theban priests who sought to make Amen the greatest deity in all of Egypt was a threat to both. Because only the priests of Thebes possessed the power to interpret the will of Amen— and whatever was the will of Amen, at least in Thebes, was the law. This threat was too much for Thutmose's successor, Amenhotep III, so he shifted his loyalty, in part, toward Ra, the chief god of Annu in Lower Egypt. In another act of political expediency and wisdom similar, to Narmer the first Pharaoh, Amenhotep III, renamed the deity Amen-Ra. This was an attempt to appease the exceedingly more powerful priests of Thebes and the people of Upper Egypt.

The new name and its association with Ra as the chief deity, however, exalted Amen to an even higher esteem among the people. Now, Amen-Ra is chief deity of Thebes, Egypt and the one and only creator of the world. He was not only a deity, but now considered the one and only deity. The view of Amen-Ra as the one and only deity was a crucial step toward Akhenaten's monotheism. Therefore, monotheism establishes itself in Egypt because of an accumulation of historical and political events, that began with the first unification of Egypt, by the Pharaoh Narmer, as mentioned above.

Inter-marriage in the royal family was a common practice because royal protocol suggests that any heir to the throne must be born from a royal princess. Nevertheless, Amenhotep III also married a Nubian wife, Tiye who was the daughter of Yuya (Joseph), the Nubian and vizier of Egypt.

At the time of the marriage, the Nubian population continued to grow in Egypt, while Yuya and his daughter Queen Tiye became more powerful and influential. This power and influence would include the preference for the stellar deity Horakhte, which was the Nubian equivalent to Ra. This was a threat to the Theban priesthood and their god Amen.

When Queen Tiye became pregnant, the Theban priests feared that the child would ascend to the throne and exert even more Horakhte (stellar deity) influence in Egypt. They proclaimed that the child could not rightfully ascend the throne because his mother Tiye, the Nubian, was not of royalty. Because the Theban priests feared that this would upset the royal tradition in Egypt, they threatened to kill the baby, if it were a boy. Queen Tiye, aware of the threat from the Theban priests did in fact deliver a baby boy. Because of this, she feared for his life and hid him in a basket near the bank of the Nile. She then summoned her Nubian relatives to nurse the child, Amenhotep IV (Akhenaten), in the home of her husband, the Pharaoh Amenhotep III.

This story is strikingly similar, to the biblical story of Moses. In fact, Ahmed Osman asserts in his book: *Moses and Akhenaten*, that Moses and Akhenaten were one in the same.[1] To be sure, the events in the lives of Moses and Akhenaten are strikingly similar. Why else would an Egyptian priest of Annu or ON (Moses/Akhenaten), lead a revolt of outcasts or lepers against his own government? Because an Egyptian priest would have been part of the Egyptian establishment—what would motivate him to take up with a bunch of outcasts?

As a young heir to the throne, Akhenaten also received his theological training from the temple of Annu or biblical ON. He later went against the Egyptian establishment, which angered the Theban priest as well as most of the Egyptian population. As we shall see later, after his abdication of the throne, and after the death of his son and successor Tutankhamen, the new Pharaoh Horemheb sent a group of outcast monotheistic worshippers of Aten, (Aten-monotheists) loyal to Akhenaten, to work in the rock quarries. Akhenaten eventually returned from exile and led them in a revolt.

During his reign, however, Amenhotep IV influenced by his father Amenhotep III and mother Tiye, the Nubian, redirected his loyalty from Amen-Ra to the Nubian deity Horakhte. During the co-regency with his father, Amenhotep IV renamed the solar deity, RE-Horakhte. After the death of his father, he changed the name of Re-Horakhte, to

Aten; and changed his own name from Amenhotep IV, to Akhenaten. His new name means pleasing to Aten; and to please Aten, he proclaims him the one and only deity. Moreover, Akhenaten prohibits the worship of all other gods, and orders the removal of all monuments erected in the name of Amen.

That proclamation diminished the god Amen and Amen-Ra, and defrocked the Theban priests of their lofty power, wealth, and influence. Akhenaten further usurped the powers of the Theban priests when he appointed himself the one and only prophet of Aten. Thus, he became the sole intermediary between the one and only deity, Aten, and the common people. When he destroyed the images of the Theban deity Amen, he allowed no images made of Aten. Therefore, a faith component to monotheism arose because Akhenaten was the sole intermediary or prophet, between the people and the invisible deity Aten.

Animosity turned to disdain and hatred between Akhenaten and the once powerful Theban priests. The defrocked Theban priests sought to regain their power and influence over Egypt but Akhenaten stood in their way. This is what they had feared when they ordered the killing of Akhenaten when he was only a baby.

4

Aten-Monotheism

Akhenaton's Aten-monotheists were among the group that would become known as the biblical Israelites. These Egyptians and Nubians ultimately came to worship a common deity known as Aten. As mentioned in chapter three, the Nubian people, and their deity Horakhte had a major influence on the formation of Egyptian monotheism. This is due to the Nubian presence in Egypt's eighteenth dynasty, when Nubian sun (stellar) worshippers married Egyptian Pharaohs.

Akhenaten's father Amenhotep III built a temple in Nubia in honor of the sun deity. Royal Nubian temples and tombs contained statues of Egyptian Pharaohs and dignitaries suggesting a close-knit relationship between these neighbors. During wartime, Nubians battled alongside Egyptians on occasion; and marriage between Nubians and Egyptians was a common occurrence, even among royalty. Prominent Nubian immigrants in Egypt during the eighteenth dynasty included Yuya and his daughter, Queen Tiye, who would later marry the Pharaoh, Amenhotep III as aforementioned.

The Nubian and Egyptian followers of Aten formed a congregation in Egypt, during Akhenaten's monotheist revolution, and ultimately became what, for the purpose of this book, we label the Aten-monotheists. This group of Aten-monotheists would eventually suffer the wrath of the Theban priests who sought to regain their power and influence. Under mounting pressure from an increasingly angry opposition who viewed him as a heretic, Akhenaten began to build a new capitol city in honor of the deity Aten.

The new capitol later known as Armana is where Akhenaten, Nefertiti, and their children, including Tutankhaten would relocate and settle. The entire administration of workers relocated along with the royal family, from Thebes to the new capital including scribes, weavers, carpenters, masons, the military, physicians, etc.

In Amana, Akhenaten built temples in honor of Aten and continued his campaign to remove images and places of worship of the deity Amen and all other lesser deities of Egypt. Soon the Theban priests along with the common people of Egypt and perhaps some in the military ranks became angrier at this behavior and began to view Akhenaten and his followers as unbearable heretics. Hence, Akhenaten could no longer depend upon the loyalty and protection of his soldiers, who after all, were from among the common people, and most of whom did not share Akhenaten's belief in the Aten deity.

> After all, the officers, and soldiers themselves believed in the gods whose images the king ordered them to destroy, they worshiped in the temples, which they were ordered to close. A conflict arose. Aye, still the strongest man in Egypt, realized the danger – the whole Amarna family and their followers, as well as the worship of Aten, came under threat. Therefore, he understood that compromise was the wisest course to follow. However, Akhenaten's belief in one God was too deep for him to accept a return to any of the former ways. Aye therefore advised him that, in his own interest, he should abdicate in favour of the young Tutankaten and flee the country. After his departure, Aye, as Tutankaten's adviser, allowed the old temples to be reopened and the ancient gods of Egypt to be worshipped again alongside the worship of the Aten, a compromise that increased his own power, as it enabled him to pose as the saviour of both army and temple.[1]

After Akhenaten's abdication and exile, Tutankaten ascended the throne at about age ten, to become the new Pharaoh. Due to his young age, Tutankhaten would share his throne with a co-regent. Perhaps because he was a child during his reign, others pressured him to restore the traditional Egyptian pantheon of deities established prior to Akhenaten's reign. Thus, he changed his name to Tutankhamen to honor the restored deity Amen, and allowed worship of the traditional deities along- side Aten. Tutankhamen now stood between the common Egyptian population and the monotheistic followers of Akhenaten.

Although Tutankhamen appeased the commoners by allowing for the return of the traditional Egyptian orthodoxy, he secretly remained loyal to Aten. This appeasement of the non-Aten commoners by Tutankhamen perhaps precipitated his murder at Sinai, by fellow Aten-monotheists. Tutankhamen went to Mount Sinai to persuade Akhenaten and his followers to rejoin the Egyptian population and live among them in peace. The Aten-monotheists, however, interprets his plea to live among their enemies as traitorous against the deity Aten. Consequently, Tutankhamen suffered a tortuous death at the foot of Mount Sinai, inside the tabernacle Akhenaten had built.

The examination of Tutankhamen's mummy revealed that his arms and legs had been broken in many places and detached from his body. While the heads of both femurs and right humorous were broken away from the remaining bone; his head and neck were also detached from his body. From this description, it is obvious that Tutankhamen was severely tortured and lynched.² Evidence inside his tomb indicates a link between some ritual objects such as robes and gloves, and Christian ritual.³ At the time of his murder at age nineteen, his father Akhenaten still lived in exile.

After Tutankhamen's death and the death of his co-regent Aye, the military general Horemheb would assume the throne. He sought to unify the people of Egypt by outlawing monotheism. Hence, the worship of Aten was outlawed and anyone caught doing so was harshly persecuted.

The biblical Hebrew sect stems from this monotheism which Pharaoh decreed unlawful. This group secretly held to the monotheistic belief in one deity, and remained loyal to the exiled King, Akhenaten. When they did remain loyal, they did so under great peril. Horemheb had not only outlawed the worship of Aten; he outlawed the very mention of Akhenaten's name under penalty of death:

> The bitterness that divided the country at this period is indicated by the actions of Horemheb, who is to be looked upon as the biblical Pharaoh of the Oppression. Worship of the Aten was abolished. The names of the Amarna kings were excised from king lists and monuments in a studied campaign to try to remove all traces of their rule from memory, and it was forbidden on pain of death even to mention the name Akhenaten.

Therefore, his followers referred to him as *MOS*, a term used in Egyptian legal cases at this period to signify the rightful son or heir.[4]

They worshiped in secret; but they could not remain completely secret, and thus suffered the wrath of Horemheb. This was the beginning of the Hebrew oppression. Later, due to their suffering and oppression under Horemheb because of their beliefs, the Aten-monotheists began to develop a messianic character. They hoped that Aten would appear one day to free them from the yolk of the Pharaoh Horemheb.

The Aten-monotheists sought to rewrite their own story and to separate themselves in some way from other Egyptians. It was the common knowledge of the ancient historians, however, that the Hebrew were from among the Egyptians. Later, the Egyptians who remained loyal to Aten joined with others, to become the biblical Hebrews.

According to Manetho, the Egyptian Historian, lepers, nomadic shepherds and the polluted were among a group purged from society and sent to work in the rock quarries on the east bank of the Nile. Included with this group were priests afflicted with leprosy.[5] Moses was not one of the priests with leprosy, but he did lead this group in a revolt. Keep in mind that every Pharaoh was also an initiate into the priesthood.

It was at this time that Akhenaten, after the death

of his son Tutankhamen, returned from exile to regain his throne; after all, his loyal followers considered him the *Mos*, or rightful heir. However, the new Pharaoh at the time was not willing to relinquish his throne so easily; consequently, Akhenaten led his loyal followers, outcasts, lepers and nomadic shepherds, on a revolt against the Egyptian establishment. Ultimately, Pharaoh's army chased Akhenaten and most of his loyal followers, including lepers and outcasts, across a narrow inlet of the Red Sea to Sinai, and eventually to Palestine.

The term leper in general, means outcast, and ancient Egyptians perhaps had a fear and contempt of lepers of all types, including outcast shepherds. The allegory of Cain and Abel describes the age-old conflict between Cain the settled farmer who murdered Abel the nomadic shepherd, in his crop field. This biblical story is also allegory for the settled Egyptians who were constantly defending their lands against nomadic invaders like the foreign Hyksos who invaded and occupied Lower Egypt for nearly one hundred years. Thus, they held contempt toward all nomadic herders and shepherds and placed them in the same outcast category as lepers.

The lepers, nomadic shepherds and polluted individuals would soon find a sympathetic ally among the native Egyptian Aten-monotheists. Although accepted by the Aten-monotheists, nomadic shepherds were obviously a less refined group relative to the native Egyptians and Nubians.

In his attempt to regain his throne, Akhenaten welcomed anyone willing to follow him. Some of them were in desperate need of law; some of them were the progeny of the first astronomers.

Nabta Playa, Nubi,a and Egypt

How did Africans come to understand the concept of night and day as it relates to the lunar calendar? As aforementioned, Nabta Playa was at one time a basin in the Nubian desert of Africa. There, archaeologists discovered fragments of ancient pottery, standing megalith stones and smaller stones arranged in a circular pattern. Cultural artifacts from the area were carbon dated from 10,000 BC to 6,000 BC. Thomas Brophy, an astrophysicist, undertook an astronomical study of Nabta Playa. He used software to track the movement of the stars over thousands of years. He observed, in an accelerated period through computer simulation, what took African people thousands of years to accomplish. Because of his study, he was able to decode the stone circle and nearby megaliths. The stone circle was actually a Calendar Circle and observatory that the Africans used to track the constellation of Orion. Part of the Calendar Circle included three stones positioned on the ground in the same pattern as Orion's belt:

> The natural place to stand when using the Calendar Circle as an observatory or

> observing diagram is at the north gate looking south— that is, toward the south meridian of the sky. By mentally registering the image of the nearest set of three upright stones inside the Calendar Circle and then looking up at the sky, the observer in circa 4800 BC would have seen the three stars of Orion's belt in almost exactly the same configuration. In other words, the three upright stones on the ground are a representation of the three stars of Orion's belt in the sky.[6]

Later, Africans constructed the three Great Pyramids on earth in a pattern mimicking the same three stars of Orion's belt:

> The correlation between the three stars of Orion's belt and the three pyramids of Giza was striking, if only for one reason: Orion's belt is made up of two bright stars and a less bright third star. This last is slightly offset to the left of the extended alignment created by the two other stars, much the same way that the third, smaller pyramid is slightly offset from the other two.[7]

This common astronomical tradition dates back thousands of years. It is undeniable proof that Africans were the first astronomers, and that Nabta Playa was the first and oldest astronomical site in world history. It follows then, that Africans also wrote the first books on astronomy, such as the *Egyptian Astronomical Texts*; and invented the first clock, a timepiece based on tracking the motion of stars. This information is significant if humanity is to achieve some semblance of reconciliation toward Africa by restoring her to her proper place in world history and by acknowledging her historical achievements and contributions that originated civilization:

> ...the information locked in the arrangement and alignments of the Calendar Circle stones and its partner stone monuments could completely change our views on the origins and racial roots of the world's greatest civilization.[8]

The stone megaliths and Calendar Circle of Nabta Playa were much smaller in scale when compared to the Great Pyramids of Giza and the Nubian Pyramids; and the Nubian pyramids were smaller in scale when compared to the Giza Pyramids. Although, there were some 200 pyramids constructed in Nubia, which was far more than the number in Egypt. This suggests a progression in stone megalith construction, pyramid architectural mathematics and perhaps religious philosophy, with the migration of the culture; from the older Nabta Playa stone structures in the Nubian Desert, east into Nubia along the Nile Valley and north along the Nile Valley into Egypt.

Current research in population Genetics affirms this movement of culture, suggesting that there has been a significant south to north gene-flow through the Nile valley, from Nubia to Egypt. For example, the ram headed criosphinxes throughout Nubia, according to the Nubians and others were precursors to the Great Sphinx of Egypt. This is further evidence of the south to north cultural and genetic-flow.

The cycle of the star Sirius, which has a rising that coincided with the sun every 1,461 years, is the basis for the invention of the lunar calendar.[9] Since we now know that it requires perhaps seven thousand years of observation of Sirius to acquire information accurate enough to develop a lunar calendar, we can simply add that amount to 4,236 BC, to arrive at circa 12,000 BC. Circa 12,000 BC is the period when the Nabta Playa basin in the Nubian Desert, began to populate with people. Later, they would construct the Stone Calendar Circle, which according to Thomas Brophy, is carbon dated to 6400 BC.

Before the African astronomers began their migration eastward toward the Nubian Nile, in search of an alternative source of water, and north along the Nile Valley into Egypt, they mastered the astronomical phenomenon of precession. The sun crosses the plane of the earth's equator twice a year, on September 23 and March 21. However, as the earth spends on its axis, the axis also moves slightly, which causes a slow westward movement of the equinoxes, and their arrival slightly earlier each year. This is precession, and the Nabta Playa Africans,

> ...were aware of precession and even tracked its effect more than three millennia before the Greeks were supposed to have discovered it. Clearly, the people of Nabta Playa were anything but primitive.[10]

This is the astronomical evidence that the Nabta Playa Nubians and later, Egyptians, tracked the celestial bodies for thousands of years, in order to eventually develop the lunar calendar that we know of today. There is no evidence, however, that the ancient Hebrews developed a calendar, which is an astronomical invention, independent and outside of the south to north cultural and genetic-flow from Nabta Playa into Nubia, through the Nile valley, into Egypt. In other words, the ancient Hebrew, because they themselves were from among the indigenous Egyptians and Nubians, derived their so-called Hebrew calendar from the Egyptian calendar.

Finally, there is a common religious tradition of spiritual salvation, resurrection of the soul and monotheism. In the Old Testament, God requested animal sacrifices from the Hebrew people. Evidence suggests that the Nabta Playa Africans engaged in ritualistic animal sacrifice as well. A mass grave of the bones of cattle indicates that the people viewed this animal with some spiritual and cultural significance. In Egypt, the bones of a bull existed inside the tomb of one of the Great Pyramids. In the Bible, when Moses returned from the mount with the tables containing the Ten Commandments, he discovered that Aaron the priest fashioned a golden calf alter.

Because it was important to the sustenance of life, the Nabta Playas, Nubians, Egyptians and Aten-monotheists placed a high value on cattle. In fact, the Africans at Nabta Playa sculpted a ten-ton stone in the shape of a cow and buried it beneath the stone megaliths near their astronomical sites. The Cow Stone, a famous artifact, is now inside the Nubian Museum. The Nubians also buried their dead with sacrificial animals, and tools such as archery equipment and axes. This further indicates a shared religious belief between Nubians and Egyptians, in a spiritual afterlife.

The belief in a spiritual afterlife and practice of burying the dead eventually led to mummification and the construction of some two hundred Nubian pyramids, and the Great Pyramids in Egypt. On the contrary, nomadic people, due to their migratory nature, traditionally burned their dead instead of burying them. Therefore, the nomadic practice of burning the dead is counter to the belief in a spiritual afterlife. Nomadic shepherds, alone, would not have been spiritually sophisticated enough to eventually invent what we know today as monotheism.

Law of the Leper

Albinism is another example of skin conditions described in Leviticus. The descriptions indicate that Egyptians, Nubians and Aten-monotheists tolerated albinism around the time of the Exodus, circa 1350 BC. It further indicates an evolution of the understanding of albinism compared to the fear and ostracism beset upon our mythical Oyinbo and other albinos in Africa for thousands of years prior. Leviticus 13, 13:

> Then the priest shall consider: and, behold, if the leprosy have covered all his flesh, he shall pronounce him clean that hath the plague: it is all turned white: he is clean.

The description of leprosy as being *white as snow*, in most cases, meant albinism, and considered clean. Whenever the leprous condition passed down genetically from seed to seed, to the following generations, it is the condition of albinism, such as the case with Gahazi. II Kings 27:

> Where the leprosy of Naaman shall cleave unto thee, and unto thy seed forever. And he went out of the presence a leper as white as snow.

II Kings 5, 1:

> Now Naaman, captain of the host of the king of Syria, was a great man with his master, and honorable, because by him the lord had given deliverance unto Syria: he was also a mighty man in valour, but he was a leper.

This passage would indicate that Naaman was an albino because any other contagious condition of leprosy would not have allowed him to achieve greatness and honor. Hence, Naaman was a leper, not an outcast. Outcasts were most likely contagious with unclean leprosy.

> According to the Egyptian priest and historian, Manetho, among the people who were sent to the east bank of the Nile to work on the rock quarries, were priests who were lepers.[11]

The priests (followers of Akhenaten's religion) who studied at the college of ON must have been albinos, because a priest could not study there, with unclean or contagious leprosy.

Flavius Josephus, the Jewish writer, took issue with Manetho's assertion that some of the priests sent to work in the rock quarries were lepers. Josephus mistakenly assumed that among the priest that Manetho referred to as lepers was Moses:

> ...there are lepers in many nations, who yet are in honor, and not only free from reproach and avoidance, but who have had the privilege of entering into holy places and temples; so that nothing hindered, but if either Moses himself or the multitude that was with him, had been liable to such a misfortune in the color of his skin, he might have made laws about them for their credit and advantage, and have laid no manner of difficulty upon them.[12]

The condition of albinism occurs with more frequency in Africa, than anywhere else, with a ratio of one in every 10,000 births. Therefore, the biblical terms leper, leprous and leprosy in many cases referred to the condition of albinism.

In the Bible, Moses complained to the Lord that the people of Israel would not believe that he was relaying the Lord's message to them because the Lord had not appeared in front of them. The lord taught Moses how to turn his rod into a serpent, and how to turn his skin from black to white, and back to black again. Exodus 4-7:

> And the Lord said furthermore unto him, put now thine hand into thy bosom. And he put his hand into his bosom: and when he took it out, behold, his hand was leprous as snow. And he said, put thine hand into thy bosom again. And he put his hand into his bosom

> again; and plucked it out of his bosom, and, behold, it was turned again as his other flesh

When Moses' sister Miriam and his brother Aaron spoke against Moses because he married an Ethiopian (Nubian) woman, and questioned why the lord only spoke with Moses and not them, the Lord became angry and punished Miriam by turning her white. Numbers 12, 10:

> And the anger of the Lord was kindled against them; and he departed. And the cloud departed from off the tabernacle; and, behold her was leprous, white as snow: and Aaron looked upon Miriam, and, behold her was leprous.

In regards to this leprous condition which turned the skin as white as snow, one can be positively certain that the home-born Hebrew such as Moses, Aaron and Miriam were not white to begin with. Because a punishment or affliction, which caused the skin to become as white as snow, indicates that Moses, Aaron, and Miriam were not originally white. Otherwise, what would be the sin or punishment of turning Miriam white as snow and causing Aaron to beseech the Lord to reconsider the laying of the sin upon her, if Miriam were already as white as snow to begin with? What would be the miracle of Moses hand becoming white if it were already white?

Anyone may arrive at the wrong conclusion, in view of the renaissance paintings and Hollywood movies and docudramas, that all Egyptians, Nubians and original Hebrews are SLC24A5 types. Yet, anyone in his right mind, looking at the Great sphinx will tell you that it is the face of an African. Anyone in his right mind who looks at the statues, sculptures, monuments, and temple art will tell you that they see African people. The lips, the eyes, the nose, the cheekbones, the braids, and the corn-rows are the features and hairstyles of Africans.

But many Egyptologists consented to the absurd that some of Ham's children such as Egyptians and Nubians, were white people with black skin. This is how far they have deluded themselves as well as others, to get around the fact that the originators of civilization were Black. Yet, the Greek historian, Strabo describes the Jews as originally coming from Egypt. Of course, this means if the Egyptians and Nubians are Black, then the original Hebrews were Black also:

> The Egyptians are especially careful in raising all their children and circumcise the boys and even the girls, a custom common to the Jews, a people originally from Egypt, as we observed when we discussed that subject.[13]

There is also evidence of a south to north genetic-flow, from the African interior, eastward to Nubia and northward to Egypt, through the Nile valley. Finally, there is the shared sculpture style, science, mathematics, architecture, art, religion, and practice of astronomy, which gave rise to the invention of the calendar. Hence, it is implausible to portray Moses, Miriam, and many other characters of the Old Testament as white SLC24A5 gene types.

5

Deception

Manetho was an Egyptian high priest and historian. He lived and studied at Annu, which is ON of the Bible, during the reign of Ptolemy II in the 3rd century BC. He authored several books, but the work entitled Aegyptiaca, written in Greek, is without a doubt his most famous and influential work. The historical work titled Aegyptiaca, was an historical account of Egypt from the first dynasty in 3100 BC to the last, around 300 BC. The work included a detailed King's list, divided into dynastic periods, along with important historical events such as the invasion and expulsion of the Hyksos or the Egyptian historical account of the biblical Exodus. No original copies of

Manetho's Aegyptiaca exist today since it was perhaps one of the 700,000 books destroyed in the fire of the Royal Library of Alexandria in 390AD. Unfortunately, for this reason, there exist only interpretations of Manetho's work by writers such as Flavius Josephus.

Flavius Josephus was born in Jerusalem during the first century CE, about 300 years after Manetho, and is the so-called father of Jewish antiquity. He authored many books about the so-called Jewish antiquity including perhaps his most influential ones: *Against Apion* and *Jewish Antiquities*. In *Against Apion*, he writes:

> ...our Jewish nation is of very great antiquity...and had a distinct subsistence of its own originally...Those antiquities contain the history of five thousand years, and are taken out of our sacred books, but are translated by me into the Greek tongue.[1]

In both books, he attempts to use Manetho and others to back his assertion that the Jewish nation was from a great antiquity. In *Against Apion*, he also writes:

> I shall begin with the writings of the Egyptians; not indeed of those that have written in the Egyptian language, which it is impossible for me to do. But Manetho was a man who was by birth an Egyptian; yet had

> he made himself master of the Greek learning, as is very evident, for he wrote the history of his own country in the Greek tongue, by translating it, as he saith himself, out of their sacred records...[2]

In fact, Flavius Josephus misinterpreted Manetho's account of the expulsion of the Hyksos as being the biblical Exodus, which would influence biblical scholars for centuries to follow. As forementioned, Flavius Josephus was not thrilled with Manetho's assertion that lepers were among the mixed multitude later known as the biblical Hebrews, with an Egyptian priest as their leader. Why would Flavius Josephus be unhappy about a historian's account of the events in his own country? For one, he did not wish to associate the Egyptians (whom he considered the enemies of the Jews) as the fathers of the Jewish people, hence, their philosophy and religion. Therefore, with his desire to distance himself from all things Egyptian, he was indeed motivated to conclude that the expulsion of the Hyksos was the actual Exodus. This is what Ahmed Osman writes in this regard, speaking of Josephus:

> ...What helped him to make the mistake was his desire to show that the Israelites had left Egypt long before Amenhotep III and the religious revolution that began in his reign...[3]

The religious revolution, which Osman refers to, is none other than Akhenaten's invention of monotheism. Not coincidently, that religious upheaval in Egypt occurred at the time of the biblical Exodus. Unfortunately for Josephus, the expulsion of the Hyksos (1550 BC) took place before the universally agreed upon time of the biblical Exodus (circa 1350 BC); hence, his history rests upon a mythical foundation. Nevertheless, he continued to assert his position that the Jews were not of Egyptian origin, which was contrary to the common belief during his time. This was something that offended him greatly, the idea of being associated with the cursed sons of Ham, who worshipped, as he says, such animal gods as the ox and others. He also had animosity toward the Greeks who did not mention the Jewish people in their historical writings.

It is likely, however, that the Greeks did not recognize the indigenous Egyptian Aten-monotheists as separate from the rest of the native Egyptians. In any event, he attacked Manetho, whenever Manetho's account of the Exodus was not in accordance with his view of the Jewish origin; he also challenged other writers such as Lysimachus and Cheremon, both of whom wrote stories like Manetho, regarding the so-called Exodus and Jewish origins. Regarding Manetho's description of the lepers and polluted sent to work in the rock quarries, Josephus writes in *Apion*:

> Now thus far he followed his ancient records; but after this he permits himself, in order to appear to have written what rumors and reports passed abroad about the Jews, and introduces incredible narrations, as if he would have the Egyptian multitude, that had the leprosy and other distempers, to have been mixed with us, as he says they were, and that they were condemned to fly out of Egypt together...[4]

Josephus praises the accuracy of Manetho's writing when there was something he liked about it; however, when Manetho describes the lepers and polluted people as being among the people who worked at the rock quarries during the reign of a Pharaoh named Amenophis (Amenhotep), Josephus dismisses it as lies and fantasy. Josephus claimed that Amenophis (Amenhotep) was not a real Pharaoh but a fantastical figment of Manetho's imagination. Further, Josephus makes a mockery of Manetho's assertion that a king named Amenophis (Amenhotep) desired to see the gods. A prophet informed him that as a precondition to seeing the god, he must purge from Egypt all the lepers and polluted people. In this regard, Josephus writes:

> What gods, I pray, did he desire to see? If he meant the gods whom their laws ordained to be worshipped, the ox, the goat, the

crocodile, and the baboon, he saw them already; but for the heavenly gods, how could he see them, and what should occasion this his desire?[5]

Here Josephus admits his ignorance of Egyptian philosophy, teachings, and religious Mystery System or perhaps he intentionally omits his knowledge of them through the distortion of facts. He himself admits that the sacred Egyptian writings were inaccessible to him due to his lack of knowledge of the Egyptian language and their hieroglyphic documentation. This is the reason he relied upon Manetho, the Egyptian who translated the sacred writings of the Egyptians into Greek, which Josephus could understand. Therefore, he was unaware that the Egyptians were the first people ever to contemplate the idea of salvation, and were the authors of history's first religious book in 4000 BC: *The Book of the Dead,* which contains within it these Negative Confessions:

The Negative Confessions:

(1) I have not done iniquity.
(2) I have not robbed with violence.
(3) I have not stolen.
(4) I have done no murder; I have done no harm.
(5) I have not defrauded offerings.
(6) I have not diminished oblations.
(7) I have not plundered the god.

(8) I have spoken no lies.
(9) I have not snatched away food.
(10) I have not caused pain.
(11) I have not committed fornication.
(12) I have not caused shedding of tears.
(13) I have not dealt deceitfully.
(14) I have not transgressed.
(15) I have not acted guilefully.
(16) I have not laid waste the plowed land.
(17) I have not been an eavesdropper.
(18) I have not set my lips in motion (against any man).
(19) I have not been angry or wrathful except for a just cause.
(20) I have not defiled the wife of any man.
(21) I have not polluted myself.
(22) I have not caused terror.
(23) I have not transgressed.
(24) I have not burned with rage.
(25) I have not stopped any ears against the words of right and truth.
(26) I have not worked grief.
(27) I have not acted with insolence.
(28) I have not stirred up strife.
(29) I have not judged hastily.
(30) I have not multiplied my words exceedingly.
(31) I have done neither harm nor ill.[6]

When the French Egyptologist Chamomel visited the Egyptian monuments, he brought with him Manetho's King lists, which enabled him to decipher the code of the hieroglyphics. This in turn allowed writers such as E.A. Wallis Budge, to translate the Egyptian holy book of spiritual salvation, *Book of the Dead,* and reveal the scared religious teachings.

Josephus may not have liked Manetho's account that Moses was a priest at Annu (ON), but if he were able to comprehend Egyptian hieroglyphs, he would have noticed the similarity between Moses' Ten Commandments and the Egyptian Negative Confessions, which were written in 4000 BC. Further, during the time of Josephus in the first century CE, he must have been aware of the so-called heretic Pharaoh Akhenaten's monotheism and of his belief in the hidden god, Aten.

Because of the hidden Aten, Akhenaten introduced a faith component to monotheism, hence, monotheism went far beyond the visible ox, goat, crocodile, or baboon that Josephus described. The invisible god of the heavens during Akhenaten's monotheism was Aten. So Aten is the first name for God, in the monotheistic religions.

Moreover, in Josephus's desire to become distant from this Egyptian monotheism, and equal desire to connect to a nation somewhere, he embraced Mesopotamia, which he believed to be the original home of the Hyksos. Again, Josephus had mistaken the Hyksos as the people of the exodus. Nevertheless, Josephus's writings became attractive to the biblical scholars of his day, because they themselves were interested in the history of the

Jewish people. Perhaps this is where the concept of *the chosen people* began to take root.

Josephus had already become agitated by any historian or writer of his day or before his day, such as Manetho, who did not conform to his view of the so-called Jewish antiquity. And by claiming Mesopotamia, he believed erroneously, that he could establish superiority over the Egyptians. For example, he contends that the Jewish people by way of Abraham introduced the Egyptians to mathematics and astronomy. This is what Josephus wrote in his book, *Jewish Antiquities*:

> ...He communicated to them arithmetic, and delivered to them the science of astronomy; for, before Abram came into Egypt, they were unacquainted with those parts of learning; for that science came from the Chaldeans into Egypt, and from thence to the Greeks also.[7]

The part he got right was that the Greeks learned astronomy from the Egyptians. Josephus mistakenly assumed that Abraham brought the knowledge of astronomy into Egypt, because he was unaware of the fact that the Africans of Nabta Playa began to track the celestial skies circa 12,000 BC, and developed the stellar stone Calendar Circle and observatory in 6400 BC. Africans followed this astronomical discovery with the invention of the lunar calendar in 4236 BC.

He also must have been unaware that the length of time that is necessary to accumulate enough data to invent a lunar calendar is about 7,000 years. Further, perhaps he was unaware of the fact that these Africans studied astronomy for thousands of years before Mesopotamia came into being. These astronomers left the evidence in their monuments such as the Great Pyramids of Giza and the stone Calendar Circle and observatory at Nabta Playa, which is now in the Nubian Museum. Josephus apparently did not know that Africans constructed these monuments in a pattern on the earth in alignment with the three stars of Orion's belt. Where is the proof from Josephus that Abraham mastered astronomy?

Nimrod the son of Cush founded a Black kingdom in Mesopotamia known as Babylon. Chaldea and Ur, the home of Abraham, was also in Mesopotamia. When Nimrod's kingdom was of one Cushitic language, the Black people constructed buildings in the tradition of the African architects, including a famous tower, (African astronomical observatory). Later, the Assyrians came into Babylon and brought with them their own language. This new language of the Assyrians caused confusion in Babylon because the original language of Babylon was Cushitic, as Nimrod was Cushitic. That confusion in language or babel, became the namesake of the astronomical tower built by Africans—the allegorical Tower of Babel.

Therefore, if there was any knowledge of

astronomy in Mesopotamia, Nimrod introduced it, as he brought it with him from Cush. Cush is the original name for Nubia, a son of Ham, as was Nabta Playa, Canaan, Phut and Egypt.

Africans were the first and oldest astronomers on earth and inventors of mathematics and authors of the oldest mathematical document known to man. Therefore, the notion of Abraham having introduced mathematics and astronomy into Egypt is blatantly false.

The interbreeding between the Assyrians and the Cushitic Africans of Mesopotamia produced a mixed Semitic type. Cushitic Africans also founded Arabia and interbred with the Joktanite that came later—the mixture between them produced the Semitic-Arab. This was also the case with Cushitic Palestine and Phoenicia.

Yet, Josephus, in his zeal to find a Jewish antiquity apart from Egypt, began his deception. It is during this time that biblical scholars along with Josephus began to argue about who started the earliest civilization on earth. And Josephus believed that the Jews were somehow the envy of the Egyptians and others, because of, among other things, there standing as the so-called chosen people of God. And that the Egyptians, Canaanites and Nubians were all cursed sons of Ham, the father of the so-called Hamitic people, meaning Black people.

With this, Josephus assumed who were the chosen people of God; who had the first and oldest civilization; and who would become the cursed bad guys in all of this. Writers and historians of Josephus's time, such as Pliny, began to describe Africans in a negative way. The Roman occupation in combination with the writings of revisionist historians such as Josephus and Pliny made the climate ripe for the manipulation and revision of history, and the mythology, which would find its place.

Deception, for the most part, is the result of some deficiency. Hence, Josephus's deception was the result of his desperate attempt to find a so-called Jewish Antiquity, which did not exist apart from Egypt. We hear nothing about Aten from the so-called biblical scholars, nor do you hear about the trinity of Isis, Osiris, and Horus. We hear nothing of the Negative Confessions (many of which are identical to Moses' Ten Commandments) or of Akhenaten's monotheism, which he developed during the time of the biblical Exodus. We hear nothing about the first and oldest holy book, the *Book of the Dead*, authored in 4000 BC. We hear nothing of the Egyptian Mystery System, which was a pathway toward salvation and the first religious system the world had ever known. Flavius Josephus and others of his day ignored all of this. Instead of illuminating Aten, they journeyed down the path of deceit and deception.

Flavius Josephus mistakenly equated the Hyksos with the Israelites of the Exodus when the Pharaoh Ahmose defeated and expelled them out of Egypt.

He also claimed that Amenhotep was a fictionalized character invented by Manetho. These mistakes alone should have discredited Josephus's contribution to biblical scholarship during the first century CE; instead, it was the beginning of the manipulation and revision of history. Perhaps Josephus influenced the authorship and editorials of the New Testament. For example, Josephus was the first writer to refer to and transcribe the names Joshua (Ye-ho-shua) or Jesua (Ye-shua), by their Greek form—Jesus.

> Now it was about this time Jesus, a wise man, if it be lawful to call him a man, for he was a doer of wonderful works—a teacher of such men as receive the truth with pleasure. He drew over to him both many of the Jews, and many of the Gentiles. He was Christ and when Pilate, at the suggestion of the principal men amongst us, had condemned him to the cross, those that loved him at the first did not forsake him, for he appeared to them alive again the third day, as the divine prophets had foretold these and ten thousand other wonderful things concerning him; and the tribe of Christians, so named from him, are not extinct at this day.[8]

It seems that when Josephus's wrote the *Jewish Antiquities,* he relied heavily on what was in the Old Testament, as he himself stated that the book would: "contain all our antiquities and the constitution of our government, as interpreted out of the Hebrew Scriptures..." However, Moses, the Egyptian, wrote allegorically, based on actual Egyptian history. After all, Moses learned all the knowledge of Egypt, including the Egyptian religion known as the Mysteries. A major teaching of the Mysteries was the salvation and resurrection of the spiritual soul. According to Josephus, prophets foretold the resurrection of Jesus while the New Testament describes the Immaculate Conception and virgin birth of Jesus.

Around 320 AD, catholic bishops voted to include the Immaculate Conception and virgin birth in the books of the Bible. What necessitated a vote on these issues by the catholic bishops, who, after all were mere men? Did they question the authenticity of the Immaculate Conception and virgin birth of Jesus? What would Christianity resemble had they not included those two stories concerning Jesus in the Bible? What was the purpose of editing out some of the other stories of the Bible, three and four hundred years later? To what extent did Josephus's writings influence the edited versions of the New Testament?

The Roman occupation of Egypt in 32 BC, contributed to Africa's marginalization for many years to come. Later, the Roman emperors Theodosius and Justinian issued edicts to prohibit the Egyptian Mystery system in the fourth and sixth centuries AD; moreover, Christianity would come under Roman control and flourish in its stead.

During the time of Josephus in the first century CE and thereafter, the Roman relocation of the ancient, traditional trade routes would further marginalize Africa. The free flow of knowledge, information, and goods, via trade routes, came to a halt. As a result, we know little about the African religion, which influenced Christianity, and little about the African historian Manetho.

Phenotypes

As mentioned above, Africans are the first and original modern humans—the one and only phenotype of modern humans; they were people of color, capable of producing melanin. Later, one phenotype became three phenotypes. The two additional phenotypes developed because of the mutated gene, SLC24A5. Original African people apparently interbred with the SLC24A5 type (whites), after their migration outside of Africa, which developed the Semitic phenotype. This is the reason that the term Semite derives from the Latin prefix, Semi, meaning half.

During antiquity, skin color was useful to describe different people, but never in any derisive or disparaging manner. For example, the Greek historian Herodotus, in his description of Egyptians, simply stated, "...Their skin was black and their hair was woolly." Certainly, the Greeks did not consider themselves superior to Egyptians and Nubians during antiquity, because they learned their philosophy, architecture, mathematics, science, astronomy, medicine, grammar and writing from them.

Yet animosity soon tainted this relationship between pupil and teacher. Soon, the Greeks and Romans would no longer esteem to be like Egyptians and Nubians but turn on them with intense dislike. Perhaps the act of invading and occupying a land, accompanied by oppression and subjugation forces the oppressor's contempt toward the subject people. Therefore, it is understandable that historians of the day would reflect such contempt in their writing. Henry Louis Gates describes the practice, which ancient writers like Pliny undertook, to disparage Africans:

> *In* the first century AD, even after direct contact with black Africans, the Roman scholar Pliny the Elder would confirm that "by report [Africans] have no heads but mouth and [eyes] in their breasts.[9]

Here, you have Pliny, during the time of Flavius Josephus and the Roman occupation of Egypt, drumming up and concurring with the negative descriptions of Africans at the time. In the first century CE, the seeds that would eventually blossom into the concept of *race* and the discontent that would accompany it, grew up in the fertile ground of the Roman occupation.

Romans practiced power and control as much as the Egyptians practiced spirituality and religion. Meaning that when it came to government and control, the Romans were fanatics. The Roman colonization of Egypt at about 32 BC was the beginning of a series of political and religious events in history that would eventually result in the modern institution of racism and white supremacy. Flavius Josephus association with the Romans is important in the context of this inquiry because key elements resulting from this association would eventually coagulate and later become essential parts of the ideology of racism.

As Herodotus once wrote, it was from Egypt that Greece and Rome came to know the deities and renamed them in their own respective languages. This should be of no surprise, as they copied and mimicked practically everything else from Africa. Later, their basic instinct to conquer, and their preoccupation with power became the impetus for Rome to abolish the African religion. This was an important act on the part of Rome, because the Egyptian Mystery System was in fact the first organized established system of spiritual salvation in the world; yet, Christianity would eventually take hold and replace it.

The abolition took place once during the reign of the Roman emperor, Theodosius in the 4th century AD, and again, by the Roman Emperor Justinian in the 6th century AD. Ironically, after Rome's abolition of the Egyptian Religion, the fledgling

Christian movement was growing even beyond the control of the Roman Empire. However, Rome came to realize that there was no better way to control the believers than by controlling the Christian church itself. With that realization, Rome reseated the Christian Coptic church in Africa, to Rome. Obviously, Rome's fanaticism with power and control, rather than any affinity for spirituality, became the impetus to reseat the church.

The relocation of the church to Rome is important in this inquiry concerning racism, because gradually over time, Christianity along with the Old Testament characters would transform and take on the look of white (SLC24A5) gene carriers. Hence, the connection between Christianity and African religion became ever more distant. Yet, Manetho records that the leader of the Exodus was a priest of ON, which means that the leader was a priest in the Egyptian Mystery System.

Because Romans used the church as a means to control the masses more efficiently, it at first enabled the Roman Empire to establish a firm foothold in its expansive territory. Eventually, however, the empire fell into decline, but what is astounding is the fact that it existed at all:

> The occupied territory under its rule expanded from Scotland to southern Egypt; and from the Euphrates River in the east, to the Atlantic Ocean in the west. In terms of ancient communication and transportation,

this swath of territory was larger than the whole earth, today.[10]

Economically, its existence was equally astounding because 90% of its population were farmers that produced barely enough for their own subsistence. Yet this population of peasant farmers supported an army and navy of 300,000 men. In turn, the Roman army and navy would exact taxes and fees from the provinces and subject states throughout its expansive territory. As a result, each Roman Emperor lived luxuriously and built elaborate temples and palaces upon the backs, so to speak, of those poor peasant farmers.[11]

This exploitive relationship between the Roman emperors and the peasant farmers would continue for the duration of the empire, between 27 BC to AD 476, with little or no unrest. This was because the Romans knew that Christianity and the idea of spiritual salvation would preoccupy the minds of the peasants and minimize the chance of unrest. Later, Christianity in the hands of Europeans in general was weaponized to conquer and colonize people throughout the world; missionaries were the hired guns in this task.

The whitewashing of Christianity and its use by the institution of racism to control and oppress people of color is even more reason to discuss the transformation of modern white Jews.

As aforementioned, Josephus worked as an interpreter for the Roman prince, Titus. In his capacity as interpreter, he convinced the Jewish residents of Jerusalem not to resist the Roman invasion. For this, many of his Jewish contemporaries viewed him as a traitor. But he was rewarded for his work, when although his given name was Joseph, the honor of a Roman name, Flavius Josephus was bestowed upon him by the Romans. Perhaps Josephus's name was not the only thing he had in common with the Romans; he also apparently looked like a Roman. This is understandable. The original Hebrew stock from Egypt intermixed with Semites and others. After the fall of Jerusalem, during the Roman occupation, some Jews dispersed to other territories, which were under the occupation of Rome. A few Jews who dispersed to Europe from Jerusalem were still essentially a Semitic half-bred people. Later, Judaism converts would settle in eastern Europe. These Judaism converts from Khazar were whites not Semites, as described in chapter six.

As mentioned above, after relocation from Egypt to Jerusalem, the original monotheists would mix and intermingle with a Semitic half-bred type. However, some original monotheists remained in Egypt, while others dispersed within Africa to such places as Ethiopia, Ghana, South Africa, and Nigeria. These original monotheists retained their natural melanin and dark complexions. A thousand years after the exodus, however, Josephus was not only a Roman subject, but perhaps lost his melanin completely and dressed like a Roman as well.

Despite the reseating of the church by Rome, and the historical misinterpretation, revision and deception of Flavius Josephus, the biblical Hebrew began in Egypt, among the Aten-monotheists. The ties are evident in the culture and tradition of the ancient Nabta Playas, Nubians, and Egyptians. Herodotus noted this regarding the Egyptian's distaste for swine:

> The pig is regarded among them as an unclean animal, so much so that if a man in passing accidentally touches the pig, he instantly hurries to the river, and plunges in with all his clothes on.[12]

Other commonalities include veneration for cattle, animal sacrifice, circumcision, tabernacles, calendars and more. The indigenous, original, ancient monotheists (Hebrew) learned all the illustrious things of the Egyptians and Nubians quite simply because they were Egyptians and Nubians.

6

African Monotheism * White Judaism

The Falasha are indigenous Hebrews from modern day Ethiopia that descended from the ancient original monotheist. In 1984, there was a political undertaking by the nation of Israel known as Operation Moses, to rescue the African Falasha Hebrews from Ethiopia. Six thousand Falasha Hebrew relocated to Israel during the process. Another 14,000 Falasha Hebrews relocated to Israel during Operation Solomon in 1999.

Falasha Hebrews, according to the myth, claims to be descendants of biblical King Solomon and the biblical Queen of Sheba. The Falasha Hebrew is distinct from the so-called conventional, European (white) Jews of Israel, according to one study conducted by Gerard Lucotte and P. Smets:

> The distinctiveness of the Y-chromosome

haplotype distribution of Falasha Jews from conventional Jewish populations (absence of haplotype VII and VIII) and their relatively greater similarity in haplotype profile to non Jewish Ethiopians (presence of heliotypes V and XI) are consistent with the view that the Falasha people descended from ancient inhabitants of Ethiopia who converted to Judaism.

This study proves that the Falasha Hebrew were indigenous to ancient Cush (Nubia/Ethiopia). However, the notion that they converted to Judaism during ancient times simply means that they were among the original Aten-monotheists.

One of Akhenaten's decrees was to disallow for the worship of any other god besides Aten. He also established rules for diet and circumcision, which are unknown to some of the lepers, nomadic shepherds, and polluted people. According to Manetho, these are among the people who would join with the home born Egyptian and Nubian monotheists.

When Akhenaten surrendered his throne to his son Tutankhamen and went into exile, the prevailing politics of the time encouraged Tutankhamen to return the Egyptian orthodox religion onto the population. This was something his father refused to do. Tutankhamen realized, though, that most of the Egyptian people did not share his belief in Aten. Therefore, he proclaimed that the traditional pantheon of gods would exist peacefully alongside the monotheistic Aten. As a result, the Theban priests regained some of their previous status. Later in his reign, the Pharaoh Tutankhamen, who remained loyal to Aten until his death, suffered a tortuous murder. At that time, Tutankhamen's father, Akhenaten, was still living in exile, while the remaining worshippers of Aten, in Egypt, suffered under suppression and persecution.

Yet, Aten worshippers remained loyal and continued to worship in secret, amongst each other, separate from the orthodox Egyptian population. Perhaps they began to use the language spoken by the Nubian members of the Aten-monotheists that further distinguished them from other common Egyptians. Initially, before Akhenaten's abdication of the throne, they sojourned with him to the new capital of Amarna. Later, some would exile to Nubia, which was a tradition among Egyptians–to seek refuge in Nubia whenever there was internal strife. Perhaps the Falasha descended from those refugees in Nubia.

This story would be consistent with Akhenaten's monotheism and religious revolution that took place during the time of the exodus. Many biblical characters represented the lives of Egyptians and Nubians during the religious revolution of the Amarna period. For example, Amenhotep III was a man of great wisdom and extraordinary genius, as was the biblical Solomon. Amenhotep III married a

Nubian woman by the name of Queen Tiye (biblical Queen Sheba). Akhenaten, the inventor of monotheism, was the son of Queen Tiye and Amenhotep III, and is represented by the biblical character, Moses. Queen Tiye was the daughter of another Nubian by the name of Yuya, who was the biblical patriarch, Joseph. Ahmed Osman, in his book, *Moses and Akhenaten*, ties those two historic figures together; hence, all other related characters along with their stories and deeds, match accordingly.

The Lemba People

DNA studies have recently linked the Lemba Jews of South Africa to the ancient Hebrews of 2500 years ago. About 80,000 Lemba Hebrews live today in South Africa and Zimbabwe. Many of them adopt Christianity but share the same cultural, Hebrew traditions as the Falasha, such as abstaining from eating pork, and the practice of circumcision. The Lemba claim to have migrated out of an ancient place called Sena into Ethiopia, from Ethiopia they continued toward their destination in South Africa. In their route to South Africa, they claimed to have settled in Zimbabwe, where they built a magnificent stone complex of walls, pathways, and buildings, which resembles the ancient stone buildings of ancient Nabta Playa, Nubia, and Egypt. According to Steve Vickers, in a BBC news story:

> The Lemba's claims mostly come from their story and their cultural and religious practices, which are said to be non-European in nature and specifically Jewish in origin. They also claim direct lineage from priestly clan known as the Bhuba clan, and these people are said to be directly related to ancient Jews Aaron and his brother Moses.

According to the bible, Moses and Aaron were home born Hebrews of Egypt and Nubia which would be joined later, on their sojourn by strangers. Perhaps some of the strangers who would later join with the home born, indigenous Aten-monotheists of Egypt and Nubia would be the Semitic type from east of the Red Sea. It is likely that Semites mixed in with the indigenous Egyptian and Nubian Aten-monotheists, instead of the other way around. Moses and Aaron were Egyptians, and Egypt was a son of Ham as was Ethiopia; hence, the Lemba Jews, who are Africans, are also descendants from the sons of Ham rather than Shem, the father of the Semites.

The practice of circumcision which we know today, to be a Jewish custom, originated with the Nubians (Ethiopians) and Egyptians, not the Semites. Herodotus, *Histories*, Book 2: 104:

> For the people of Colchis are evidently Egyptian and this I perceived for myself before I heard it from others. So, when I had

come to consider the matter, I asked them both; and the Colchians had remembrance of the Egyptians more than the Egyptians of the Colchians; but the Egyptians said they believed that the Colchians were a portion of the army of Sesostris. That this was so I conjectured myself not only because they are dark-skinned and have curly hair (this of itself amounts to nothing, for there are other races which are so), but also still more because the Colchians, Egyptians, and Ethiopians alone of all the races of men have practiced circumcision from the first. The Phoenicians and the Syrians who dwell in Palestine confess themselves that they have learnt it from the Egyptians, and the Syrians about the river Thermodon and the river Parthenios, and the Macronians, who are their neighbors, say that they have learnt it lately from the Colchians. These are the only races of men who practice circumcision, and these evidently practice it in the same manner as the Egyptians. Of the Egyptians themselves however and the Ethiopians, I am not able to say which learnt from the other, for undoubtedly it is a most ancient custom; but that the other nations learnt it by intercourse with the Egyptians, this among others is to me a strong proof, namely that those of the Phoenicians who have intercourse with Hellas cease to follow the example of the Egyptians in this matter, and do not circumcise their children.

Despite Herodotus's uncertainty, Nubians practiced circumcision first, and taught the practice to the Egyptians. The original purpose of the tradition was to separate females and males from what Africans considered gender ambiguity. Hence, Africans practiced the tradition of circumcision on both male and female. Other cultures who lack understanding, may consider the practice of female circumcision to be cruel, seemingly based on some kind of sexual control and oppression of women in a male dominated society. In truth, Africans believe that through circumcision, the male and female became more distinct and thus more complete respectively.

The practice of circumcision is also practiced by African Hebrews who settled in other parts of Africa, including: the Jewish Moors of the North and the Black Jews and Hebrews of Egypt, Ethiopia, Ghana, Angola, and Nigeria. This indicates that the original indigenous Aten-monotheists of Egypt and Nubia migrated not just east into Jerusalem, but also into the interior of Africa, west, north, and south, and took with them a shared culture and tradition such as ritualistic animal sacrifices, strict adherence to dietary standards, circumcision and more. Further, despite Operation Moses and Operation Solomon, many African Jews and Hebrews are clearly not recognized today.

Semites

The term Semite has taken on a new meaning. The original meaning stems from the Latin prefix semi, which means half. Here is a definition of semi according to the dictionary: partial, partially, somewhat, half, resembling, having some characteristics of something. This indicates that the Semitic genotype originally is a result of a mixture of indigenous Africans and white SLC24A5 gene types. We know that in Babylon the Cushitic Blacks who founded the nation eventually mixed with Assyrian immigrants to form a Semitic type. This also occurred in Arabia, when Joktanite people mixed with the original Cushitic Blacks that founded it. Phoenicia and Palestine were also initially Black Cushitic nations that later became Semitic because of interbreeding. Today, Webster dictionary gives this definition for Semite: a member of any of the peoples speaking Semitic languages. Webster's definition of Semitism is quite different:

> A Semitic characteristic, a Semitic expression or idiom, ideas, cultural ideas, etc., thought of as essentially Jewish.

Since Webster refers to Semitism as anything essentially Jewish, it excludes Christians, Moslems and others who may also happen to speak a Semitic language. This confusion in the definition of the word by Webster dictionary is a great example of words that have lost their original meaning. The convoluted definitions from Webster, for the term Semite or Semitism, are problematic, to say the least. The Falasha Hebrews originally spoke a Cushitic (Nubian) language whereas today they speak Amharic, which is Semitic. Some Falasha Ethiopians that relocated to Israel are adopting Hebrew as their new language. And the white Jews of Europe are considered more Semitic than others by virtue of Webster's definition associating Semitism with anything Jewish.

Some white Jews, many of whom are not originally Semitic themselves, accuse Palestinians, who are Semitic and speak a Semitic language, with anti-Semitism. The reason Webster dictionary defines Semitism as anything essentially Jewish is because the term anti-Semitism was first used to describe Nazi Germany's anti-Jewish genocide; and the establishment of Israel was a result of that. Therefore, the term Semite has essentially taken on a new meaning. Instead of Semi-meaning half-bred or mixed genotype of the children of Shem, it has become associated with the modern-day white Jew.

This confusion is perhaps the reason that Hitler, in his final solution toward a so-called white master race decided to exterminate the Jews, Gypsies and all other mixed race half-bred people in Germany and other parts of German occupied Europe. He apparently understood the term Semite to mean a mixed or half-bred, mulatto people; what he failed to understand was that many of the European Jews (who were the targets of his wrath) were white like him, a sizeable number of whom converted to Judaism during Europe's Dark Ages. In one sense the term Semite refers to language, and in another sense, it refers to the genotypic offspring of the biblical Shem, or in other words, ethnicity, or *race*.

White Jews of Europe

Khazar was a little-known empire, that existed in Europe between the seventh and twelfth centuries. The people were of Turkish stock and the territory of Khazar was in a strategically important area between the Black Sea and the Caspian. This was an important geological setting due to the following:

> It acted as a buffer protecting Byzantium against invasions by the lusty barbarian tribesmen of the northern steppes- Bulgars, Magyars, Perchenegs, etc. - and, later, the Vikings and the Russians. But equally, or even more important both from the point of view of the Byzantine diplomacy and of European history, is the fact that the Khazar armies effectively blocked the Arab avalanche in its most devastating early stages, and thus prevented the Muslim conquest of Eastern Europe.[1]

Khazar stood geographically and politically as a safeguard for Byzantine Christianity against the advancement of the Muslim Holy warriors into Eastern Europe. The wars between the Arabs and the Khazars would last nearly a hundred years. When the war was all over, a peculiar thing happened; instead of embracing Christianity, the Khazar ruling class converted to Judaism. The conversion to Judaism took place a few years after the last battle between the Khazars and Muslim warriors, around 742AD–according to Arthur Koester:

> ...the King, his court and the military ruling class embraced the Jewish faith, and Judaism became the state religion of the Khazars.[2]

The major facts regarding the Khazar conversion to Judaism, according to Koestler are beyond dispute, but regarding their dispersion after the empire's destruction, he goes on to say:

> What is in dispute is the fate of the Jewish Khazars after the destruction of their empire, in the twelfth or thirteenth century. On this problem the sources are scant, but various late mediaeval Khazar settlements are mentioned in the Crimea, in the Ukraine, in Hungary, Poland and Lithuania. The general picture that emerges from these fragmentary pieces of information is that of a migration

of Khazar tribes and communities into those regions of Eastern Europe - mainly Russia and Poland - where, at the dawn of the Modern Age, the greatest concentration of Jews were found. This has led several historians to conjecture that a substantial part, and perhaps the majority of eastern Jews - and hence of world Jewry - might be of Khazar, and not of Semitic origin.[3]

Other Jews, according to Arthur Koestler, also settled in Western Europe towards the end of the first millennium. He also contends that perhaps some of those communities had existed since the Roman days:

> ...between the destruction of Jerusalem and the decline of the Roman Empire, Jews had settled in many of the greater cities under its rule, and were later on reinforced by immigrants from Italy and North Africa.[4]

Their relatively miniscule numbers, however, could not account for the large population of white Jews in Eastern Europe, particularly Poland, which existed shortly after the fall of Khazar. According to Arthur Koester:

> ...the large majority of surviving Jews in the world is of eastern European - and thus perhaps mainly of Khazar - origin. If so, this

would mean that their ancestors came not from Jordon but from the Volga, not from Canaan but from the Caucasus, once believed to be the cradle of the Aryan race; and that genetically they are more closely related to the Hun, Uigur and Magyar tribes than to the seed of Abraham, Isaac and Jacob. Should this turn out to be the case, then the term 'anti-Semitism' would become void of meaning, based on a misapprehension shared by both the killers and their victims. The story of the Khazar Empire, as it slowly emerges from the past, begins to look like the most cruel hoax which history has ever perpetrated.[5]

Thus, the physical transformation of the First Monotheists into some white practitioners of Judaism of modern day, and modern-day portrayal of Old Testament characters as SLC24A5 gene types.

7

First Civilization

In this inquiry concerning African History, we have disproved the very tenets of the ideology since the ideology is based on the false concept of *race*. Therefore, racism, which is the belief in the innate and inherent superiority of whites over the innate and inherent inferiority of Africans, is a false ideology. We have demonstrated this through our historical investigation. Racists may argue today, however, that the relative underdevelopment of Africa is proof itself that there is indeed, a status of African inferiority. Given this argument, it is important to discuss the historical contribution and achievement of Africans on the one hand; and causes contributing to its modern-day underdevelopment—such as slavery and colonialism, on the other.

This chapter will cover the Egyptian Mystery

System—an ancient Egyptian religion, philosophy, and culture; and the subsequent abolition of the Egyptian Mystery System, by the Roman Empire, which precipitated Europe's fall into the Dark Ages. It was Europe's emergence from the Dark Ages (chapter nine) in combination with two important maritime and military innovations, which led to the European slave trade and subsequent colonization of Africa. This period of contact with whites led directly to Africa's regression into its own dark ages and consequent underdevelopment.

Stolen Legacy

In the following passage from his book *Stolen Legacy*, George James describes just how the historical achievement of the Africans in Egypt would be stolen; moreover, the theft results in the credit and glory falsely bestowed upon the Greeks for having developed Egyptian Arts, Science and philosophy:

> The term Greek philosophy, to begin with is a misnomer, for there is no such philosophy in existence. The ancient Egyptians had developed a very complex religious system, called the Mysteries, which was also the first system of salvation.
> As such, it regarded the human body as a prison house of the soul, which could be liberated from its bodily impediments,

through the disciplines of the Arts and Sciences, and advanced from the level of a mortal to that of a God. This was the notion of the summum bonum or greatest good, to which all men must aspire, and it also became the basis of all ethical concepts. The Egyptian Mystery System was also a Secret Order, and membership was gained by initiation and a pledge to secrecy. The teaching was graded and delivered orally to the Neophyte; and under these circumstances of secrecy, the Egyptians developed secret systems of writing what they had learnt.

James continues:

After nearly five thousand years of prohibition against the Greeks, they were permitted to enter Egypt for the purpose of their education. First, through the Persian invasion and secondly through the invasion of Alexander the Great. Therefore, from the sixth century B.C. to the death of Aristotle in 322 B.C., the Greeks made the best of their chance to learn all they could about Egyptian culture. Most students received instructions directly from the Egyptian priests, but after the invasion of Alexander the Great, the Royal temples and libraries were plundered and pillaged. Aristotle converted the library at Alexandria into a research center and took credit for having authored a voluminous quantity of books. But such a large number of books would have been impossible for Aristotle or any human to accomplish in one lifetime.[1]

Here we can plainly see the arrogance and greed of Aristotle who seized and plundered the Royal library, and claimed as his own, the intellectual work, which the Egyptians developed over thousands of years. James believes that the plundering and pillaging of the Royal library of Alexandria resulting in the misnomer, Greek philosophy, was like actors upon the stage, playing their respective roles:

> Greek philosophy is somewhat of a drama, whose chief actors were Alexander the Great, Aristotle and his successors in the peripatetic school, and the Roman Emperor Justinian. Alexander invaded Egypt and captured the Royal Library at Alexandria and plundered it. Aristotle made a library of his own with the plundered books, while his school occupied the building and used it as a research centre. Finally, Justinian the Roman Emperor abolished the Temples and schools of philosophy i.e. another name for the Egyptian Mysteries which the Greeks claimed as their product, and on account of

which, they have been falsely praised and honored for centuries by the world, as its greatest philosophers and thinkers. This contribution to civilization was really and truly made by the Egyptians and the African Continent, but not by the Greeks or the European Continent. We sometimes wonder why the people of African descent find themselves in such a social plight as they do, but the answer is plain enough. Had it not been for this drama of Greek philosophy and its actors, the African Continent would have had a different reputation, and would have enjoyed a status of respect among the nations of the world....Finally, the dishonesty in the movement of the publication of a Greek philosophy, becomes very glaring, when we refer to the fact, purposely that by calling the theorem of the Square on the Hypotenuse, the Pythagorean theorem, it has concealed the truth for centuries from the world, who ought to know that the Egyptians taught Pythagoras and the Greeks, what mathematics they knew.[2]

Unfortunately, this drama has played out to the detriment of Egypt and the African continent. However, the historical truth destroys the false notion that Africans are inherently inferior while Europeans are inherently superior. The ideology of racism could not be further from the truth, because Africans created the Arts and Sciences for the world. Yet, the world believes in the white supremacist lie based in part on the thievery of the Greeks:

> For centuries the world has been misled about the original source of the Arts and Sciences; for centuries Socrates, Plato and Aristotle have been falsely idolized as models of intellectual greatness; and for centuries the African continent has been called the Dark continent, because Europe coveted the honor of transmitting to the world, the Arts and Sciences.[3]

The Egyptian Mystery system

The Egyptians considered the human body to be a kind of prison house for the soul. For this reason, over thousands of years, they developed a complex religious system called the Egyptian Mystery System. The Mystery System was a pathway to salvation; that is, an elevation to a state of glory–or deity beyond the mortal human experience. The Egyptian Mystery System was the earliest theory of salvation in world history.

The method for obtaining this salvation was to achieve a balance between learning the Arts and Sciences and living a virtuous life. For the neophyte, the pathway to salvation consisted of three levels: initiation, illumination, and perfection. Upon initiation to the secret order of the Mystery System, the neophyte made a solemn pledge to keep secret his learning. The priests of the Mystery system also developed a secret language and sacred writings to safeguard the knowledge. According to James, the Egyptian Mystery System was similar, to a modern university, in that it was a leading center of organized culture, which candidates aspired to attend. The education of the neophyte according to James consisted of:

> ...the ten virtues, which were made a condition to eternal happiness, but also of the seven Liberal Arts which were intended to, liberate the soul...

James continues:

> Grammar, Rhetoric, and Logic were disciplines of moral nature by means of which the irrational tendencies of a human being were purged away, and he was trained to become a living witness of the Devine Logos. Geometry and Arithmetic were sciences of transcendental space and numeration, the comprehension of which provided the key not only to the problems of one's being; but also to the physical ones, which are so baffling today, owing to our use of the inductive methods. Astronomy

dealt with the knowledge and distribution of latent forces in man, and the destiny of individuals, races and nations. Music (or Harmony) meant the living practice of philosophy i.e., the adjustment of human life into harmony with God, until the personal soul became identified with God, when it would hear and participate in the music of the spheres. It was therapeutic, and was used by the Egyptian Priests in the cure of diseases. Such was the Egyptian theory of salvation, through which the individual was trained to become godlike while on earth, and at the same time qualified for everlasting happiness. This was accomplished through the efforts of the individual, through the cultivation of the Arts and Sciences on the one hand, and a life of virtue on the other. There was no mediator between man and his salvation, as we find in the Christian theory.[4]

A life of virtue was required for any initiate into the Egyptian Mystery System; hence, the curriculum at the Egyptian Mystery System included the following Ten Virtues as George James writes in Stolen Legacy:

> (1) Control of thought and (2) Control of action, the combination of which Plato called *Justice* (i.e., the unswerving righteousness of

thought and action). (3) Steadfastness of purpose, which was equivalent to *Fortitude*. (4) Identity with spiritual life or of higher ideals, which was equivalent to *Temperance* and attained when the individual had gained conquest over the passion (al) nature. (5) Evidence of having a mission in life and (6) Evidence of a call to spiritual Orders of the Priesthood in the Mysteries: the combination of which was equivalent to *Prudence* or of deep insight and graveness that befitted the faculty of Seer ship. Other requirements in the ethical system of the Egyptian Mysteries were: (7) Freedom from resentment, when under the experience of persecution and wrong. This was known as courage. (8) Confidence in the power of the master (as Teacher), and (9) Confidence in one's own ability to learn; both attributes being known as Fidelity. (10) Readiness or preparedness for initiation. There has always been this principle of the ancient Mysteries of Egypt: "When the pupil is ready, then the master will appear". This was equivalent to a condition of efficiency at all times for less than this pointed to a weakness.[5]

It is apparent that Plato derived his Four Cardinal Virtues: Temperance, Fortitude, Prudence, and Justice, from the Egyptian Ten Virtues, because similar in the way Moses derived his Ten

Commandments out of the nearly one hundred Negative Confessions—the lesser is derived from the greater in terms of both quantity and dates of conception. Several of Moses' Ten Commandments are identical to the Negative Confessions, which had existed for thousands of years before Moses. Moses and Plato were students at the Egyptian Mystery System, as was the likes of Socrates, Pythagoras, and others. Therefore, it is quite clear, as George James writes:

> ...that Plato drew the four Cardinal virtues from the Egyptian ten; also, that Greek philosophy is the offspring of the Egyptian Mystery System.[6]

Herodotus

George James documented in his book *Stolen Legacy* the Greek theft of Africa's arts, science and culture, but if there still be any doubt, this stolen legacy by the Greeks was also well documented by one of their own, the Greek Historian Herodotus, who is considered by the west to be the Father of History. Therefore, Herodotus, the so-called Father of History, is one of the most credible sources available. Here is what he has written regarding what the Greeks learned from the Egyptians:

> Almost all the names of the gods came into Greece from Egypt. My inquiries prove that

they were all delivered from a foreign source, and my opinion is that Egypt furnished the greater number.[7]

Herodotus confirms that the Greeks borrowed many practices from Egypt:

> Besides these, which have been mentioned, there are many other practices whereof I shall speak hereafter, which the Greeks have borrowed from Egypt.[8]

Herodotus, the so-called father of history also wrote this regarding the Egyptians as historians:

> With respect to the Egyptians, it is to be remarked that those who live in the corn country, devoting themselves, as they do, far more than any other people in the world, to the preservation of the memory of past actions, are the best skilled in history of any men that I have ever met.[9]

Herodotus also describes how Egyptians not only used medicine, but each practitioner of medicine was a specialist:

> Medicine is practiced among them on a plan of separation; each physician treats a single disorder, and no more: thus the country swarms with medical practitioners, some

> undertaking to cure diseases of the eye, others of the head, others again of the teeth, others of the intestines...[10]

Again, the Egyptians, invented the science of medicine and taught it to the Greeks, yet receive little recognition for doing so. Instead, young physicians today, take the Hippocratic Oath, named for the Greek Hippocrates. And the Greek Pythagoras is the namesake of the theorem of the Square on the Hypotenuse, despite having learned all their mathematics from the Egyptians.

And Herodotus described the Egyptians as the best and most skilled historians he had ever met. Yet, in the west, students know nothing of Manetho, the ancient Egyptian historian who wrote the Dynastic Kings list, which modern Egyptologists would be hopeless without. He also wrote several books including his most influential Aegyptiaca, the history of his native Egypt. So, the misnamed Pythagorean Theorem, Hippocratic Oath, and lack of recognition of the achievement of Egyptian historian Manetho, are symptomatic of the stolen African knowledge and discoveries.

8

First Art and Science

The curriculum of the Mystery System included the following subjects: grammar, rhetoric, logic, arithmetic, geometry, astronomy, and music. Along with spiritual principles, it was necessary for the initiate to master grammar, rhetoric, and logic to purge away their own irrational tendencies, and the irrational tendencies of others, through debate.

Before the development of the Mystery System, Africans first had to undergo the long and tedious task of discovering knowledge and technique, which led to the development of the arts and sciences. They did not simply read a book to learn about mathematics, because mathematics did not exist before their time. They did not pick up a calendar and decide that they would meet someone on a Saturday. First, they had to track the motion of the celestial bodies for thousands of years before they could invent the lunar calendar which we know today consists of 365 days and a 12-month year with a correction every fourth year. Furthermore, they did not pick up a copy of Grey's Anatomy to study medicine, because they invented medicine. The invention and discovery of medicine was essentially the result of Africans adapting to their environment in the Nile Valley, where they settled. While settlement compels a people to bury their dead, settlement in the Nile Valley, necessitated the development of the unique funerary technique of mummification.

Medicine

Besides preserving the dead in preparation for the afterlife, the mummification process also circumvented the spread of disease. Obviously, Africans were conscious of the process of disease, and enacted whatever measures necessary to avoid it. This in the case of the Egyptians, included abstinence from pork; for example, and fasting by way of purging the body from impurities for the first three days of each month. They understood the correlation between the consumption of food and disease or ill health:

> The following is the mode of life habitual to them: —For three successive days in each month they purge the body by means of emetics and clysters, which is done out of regard for their health, since they have a persuasion that every disease to which men

> are liable is occasioned by the substances whereupon they feed...they are, I believe, the healthiest people in the world...[1]

The African consciousness of disease led to the development of medicine from plants, and a system of medical practice whereby medical practitioners specialized on different ailments of the body, such as that of the eyes, skin, mouth, feet, bones, etc. Again, this quote by Herodotus bears repeating:

> Medicine is practiced among them on a plan of separation; each physician treats a single disorder, and no more: thus the country swarms with medical practitioners, some undertaking to cure diseases of the eye, others of the head, others again of the teeth, others of the intestines...[2]

This practice of medicine occurred thousands of years before the birth of Hippocrates the Greek, and so-called father of medicine. A medicine which, along with other arts and sciences developed not because of any African superiority to other men, but because of their settlement in a superior African environment, near sources of water such as lakes and great rivers such as the Nile, according to Diop:

> In the Nile valley, civilization resulted from man's adaptation to that particular milieu. As declared by the Ancients and by the

> Egyptians themselves, it originated in Nubia. This is confirmed by our knowledge that the basic elements of Egyptian civilization are neither in Lower Egypt, nor in Asia, nor in Europe, but in Nubia and the heart of Africa; moreover, that is where we find the animals and plants represented in the hieroglyphic writing...

Diop continues:

> The Egyptians usually measured the height of the flood waters with a "Nilometer", and from it they deduced the annual yield of the harvests by mathematical calculation. The calendar and astronomy also resulted from that sedentary farm life. Adaptation to the physical surroundings gave birth to certain hygienic measures: mummification (to avoid epidemics of the plague from the Delta), fasting, diets, and so on, which gradually led to medicine coming into existence. The development of social life and exchanges required the invention and use of writing. Sedentary life led to the institution of private property and a whole ethic (summarized in the questions asked of the deceased at the tribunal of Osiris). This code of ethics was the opposite of the warlike, predatory habits of the Eurasian nomads[3]

All of the fundamental arts and sciences develop during the pre-dynastic era in Egypt, awaiting the exploits of the first Pharaoh Narmer, and the genius Imhotep. Narmer set the groundwork with the unification of Upper and Lower Egypt, creating the first dynasty; this political savvy establishes cultural stability, and enables the genius Imhotep to practice medicine during Egypt's third dynasty, 2,500 years before Hippocrates. Thus, Imhotep is the true father of medicine:

> ...Imhotep treated diseases of the bone, stomach, abdomen, rectum, bladder and eyes. He detected ailments by the shape, condition and color of the visible parts of the body such as the tongue, hair, nails, and skin. He treated decayed teeth and decayed bone of the mouth, gallstones, tuberculosis, gout, appendicitis, mastoid diseases, and rheumatoid arthritis. He and his contemporaries practiced surgery, extracted medicines from plants and, like today's doctors, listened to sounds from the body's organs such as heart, lungs, and stomach. He knew the functions of the vital organs of the body and about the circulation of the blood.[4]

Egyptian Surgical Papyrus

The Egyptian Surgical Papyrus (Smith) dates to 17th century BC. It is a copy of a more ancient manuscript originally authored during the Pyramid Age of the Old Kingdom (2649-2152BC). The Surgical papyrus is thus the oldest scientific document known. It, like the Ahmose Mathematical Papyrus was a manuscript for teaching purposes. The author wrote the manuscript in practical *case* form; that is, the author presents 48 surgical cases, each followed by his Examination, Diagnosis, and Treatment.

Although the author is unknown, it is most likely the work of Imhotep, the gifted multiple genius. He was not only the father of medicine, but also a royal architect, mathematician, astronomer, scribe, and engineer. As a royal architect and engineer, he built the very first Egyptian pyramid and the world's first stone building; the Step Pyramid at Saqqara.

The Surgical Papyrus was most likely a copy of an original manuscript entitled: *Secret Book of the Physician*.[5] It is safe to assume that the title refers to Imhotep since he lived during the time of its authorship, nearly 5,000 years ago; and is the world's very first physician and rightful father of medicine.

> It was evident from our ancient treatise that our ancient surgeon, whoever he may have been, was a man of observant and discerning mind, with a wide outlook upon the life of his time. The terms which he uses...convey

the impression of a man actually involved in
the process of building up a terminology in a
field of observation...He seems to be doing
for the first time in any field of science what
has since happened in one area of scientific
observation after another.[6]

The Egyptian Surgical papyrus is evidence of the African knowledge of surgery, but also anatomy, pathology, and physiology. It is most probable that the ancient physicians practiced dissection to gain knowledge of these areas of study. Later, there were other medical papyri written about surgical instruments, anatomy, medicine, diseases, and physiology. And there was knowledge of the central nervous system with the brain and spinal column as its control centers. Through observation, the ancient African surgeons realized spinal and brain trauma could affect the movement of the body. In fact, the ancient Africans were the first to recognize this crucial body part and thus first to use a term denoting *brain*:

> For the first time in recorded human speech, our treatise contains the word "brain", which is unknown in any other language in this age, or in any other treatise of the Third Millennium B.C. The earliest discussions of the brain have hitherto been found in Greek medical documents probably over two thousand years later than our Egyptian

treatise.[7]

The Egyptians were obviously first to discover that the heart was at the center of a group of vessels that supplied blood to the human body, and thus became an important aspect of determining the general health of the patient:

> The importance of observing the action of the heart in determining the condition of the patient, appears here for the first time in medical history... there is much probability that the surgeon *counts* the strokes of the pulse, and it is doubtless a significant fact that the first physician known to have counted the pulse, Herophilos of Alexandria (born 300 B.C.), lived in Egypt. It will probably also not have been wholly accident that this was done in the land which produced the earliest known time-pieces, for Herophilos used an Egyptian water-clock for timing his count of the pulse.[8]

By now, it should be no surprise to the reader that the physician credited for having counted the pulse first, is the Greek, Herophilos; without acknowledging where the Greeks learned about medicine, and accrediting African knowledge to the Greeks. Hence, college fraternal organizations referring to themselves as Greeks; and medical students swearing the Hippocratic Oath, despite

Egyptians practicing medicine 2,500 years before the birth of Hippocrates. Greeks lived and studied in Egypt for centuries to obtain their knowledge of medicine and the arts and sciences in general:

> In the first place we have already noticed that the greatest of the Greek medical investigators, at the climax of Greek achievement in medical science in the Third Century B.C., lived in Egypt, as so many of the intellectual men of Greece had for centuries before that time traveled and studied in Egypt.[9]

In regards to Surgical Papyrus, many of the 48 cases below dealt with trauma such as fractured, punctured, and lacerated skulls, broken mandibles, broken necks, dislocated vertebrae, fractured ribs, fractured arms and legs, dislocated clavicles, broken nasal bones, and gaping and infected wounds. This type of trauma seems more reminiscent of a modern-day emergency hospital, than those that would occur in an ancient society, 5,000 years ago. However, many cases were the result of war trauma and building accidents. Not only were there injuries from the slings, arrows, swords, and battle axes of war; but also, injuries resulting from the high-rise building projects such as the temples, obelisks, bridges and pyramids that endangered the lives of thousands of construction workers. This type of trauma was therefore as common to the ancient surgeon, as gunshot wounds are to the American inner city trauma surgeon. In addition, there was specialized knowledge of conditions affecting only women and children, which for the most part not included among the following 48 cases in the Egyptian surgical papyrus. For brevity, the list below includes only the type or title of each surgical case, not their complete examination, diagnosis, and treatment.

Cases

(1) A wound in the head, penetrating the bone
(2) A gaping wound in the head penetrating to the bone
(3) A gaping wound in the head penetrating the bone and perforating the skull
(4) A gaping wound in the head penetrating the bone and splitting the skull
(5) A gaping wound in the head with compound comminuted fracture of the skull
(6) A gaping wound in the head with compound comminuted fracture of the skull and rupture of the meningeal membranes
(7) A gaping wound in the head penetrating to the bone and perforating the sutures
(8) Compound comminuted fracture of the skull displaying no visible external injury
(9) Wound in the forehead producing a compound comminuted fracture of the skull
(10) A gaping wound at the top of the eyebrow,

penetrating to the bone
(11) A broken nose
(12) A break in the nasal bone
(13) Compound comminuted fracture in the side of the nose
(14) Flesh wound in one side of the nose penetrating to the nostril
(15) Perforation of the bone in the region of the maxilla and zygoma
(16) Split of the bone in the region of the maxilla and the zygoma
(17) Compound comminuted fracture of the bone in the region of the maxilla and zygoma
(18) A wound in the soft tissue of the temple, the bone being uninjured
(19) A perforation in the temple
(20) A wound in the temple perforating the bone
(21) A split in the temporal bone
(22) Compound comminuted fracture of the temporal bone
(23) A slit in the outer ear
(24) A fracture of the mandible
(25) A dislocation of the mandible
(26) A wound in the upper lip
(27) A gaping wound in the chin
(28) A gaping wound in the throat penetrating to the gullet
(29) A gaping wound in a cervical vertebra
(30) Sprain in cervical vertebra
(31) Dislocation of cervical vertebra
(32) Displacement of a cervical vertebra

(33) A crushed cervical vertebra
(34) Dislocation of the two clavicles
(35) A fracture of the clavicle
(36) A fracture of the humerus
(37) A fracture of the humerus with rupture of overlying soft tissue
(38) A split in the humerus
(39) Tumors or ulcers in the breast, perhaps resulting from injury
(40) A wound in the breast
(41) An infected or possibly necrotic wound in the breast
(42) A sprain of the sterno-costal articulations
(43) A dislocation in the sterno-costal articulations
(44) Fractured ribs
(45) Bulging tumors on the breast
(46) Abscess with prominent head on the breast
(47) A gaping wound in the shoulder
(48) A sprain in a spinal vertebra[10]

Ahmose Mathematical Papyrus

Ahmose, the author of the mathematical papyrus and Ahmose the Pharaoh who defeated and expelled the Hyksos out of Egypt, is perhaps the same individual. As Pharaoh, Ahmose was also a trained scribe, who perhaps wanted to preserve the ancient knowledge during a time of strife. From his location in Upper Egypt, near Nubia, the Pharaoh Ahmose attacked, defeated, and expelled the foreign Hyksos from Lower Egypt; and the defeat of the foreign Hyksos and the unification of Egypt as a result, was a crucial event in Egyptian history.

Perhaps the Hyksos occupation motivated Ahmose to preserve the sacred ancient knowledge from the pillaging foreigners. Therefore, the scribe, who is perhaps the Pharaoh Ahmose, copied the mathematical papyrus from an earlier 12th dynasty (1994-1781 BC) manuscript. This means that the original author composed the mathematical document 4,000 years ago—the most ancient mathematical document known.

The Ahmose Mathematical Papyrus is an instructional text in the sense that it presents problems along with the correct calculations and solutions to the problems. The text included 84 mathematical problems. Ahmose introduced the mathematical text with the following statement:

> Accurate reckoning, for inquiring into the meaning of all things, and grasping the knowledge of all things, mysteries, and all secrets.[11]

Indeed, for these ancient Africans, mathematics was simply a means by which they solved everyday practical problems during their time. Some of the problems in the Ahmose Mathematical Papyrus are quantity or to use the Egyptian term, *aha* questions that were in the form of algebraic type linear equations. The challenge was to determine solutions to problems with unknown quantities.

Other problems had to do with distribution—the division and distribution of commodities such as bread and beer into fractional but equal portions among a given number of individuals. To know the volume of the stored grains that produced the bread and beer, however, such as wheat or barley, there had to be an accurate measurement of the geometric volume of both cylindrical and rectangular based granaries:

Problem 41
What is the volume of a cylindrical granary with a diameter of 9 height of 10?

The actual solution to this problem approximates the value of pi—3.1605.[12]

In addition, it was necessary to measure and divide rectangular, triangular and cut-off triangular pieces of land.

Problem 51
Example of making a triangle in land: If is said to thee, A triangle of khet 10 on the side of it, khet 4 in the base of it, what is the area of it?[13]

Problem 52
Example of making a cut-off triangle of land: If is said to thee, A cut-off triangle of land of khet 20 on the side of it, khet 6 in the base of it, khet 4 on the cut-off; what is the area of it?

Note: The land is a trapezoid or truncated triangle.[14]

When Nubian and Egyptian engineers constructed the pyramids, it was necessary to measure the slope as it related to its horizontal base or horizon, to assure that the four faces of the pyramid were of equal incline:

Problem 56
Example of reckoning a pyramid that has a base side of 360 and an altitude of 250. What is the seked of it?
Note: The term seked is equivalent to the cotangent of the angle of the slope of the pyramid.[15]

Egyptians discovered geometry, and used trigonometry to build their pyramids. They also calculated the value of pi at least a thousand years before the Greeks. Obviously, Africans taught geometry to Greeks such as Pythagoras, way before the time of Euclid. And obviously, Africans knew before Pythagoras the theorem of the Square on the Hypotenuse.

In practical applications, some problems required the use of the previously mentioned linear *aha* equations to determine solutions to unknown quantities. In addition, as can be seen from the sample problems above, Africans were able to calculate the area and volume of rectangular and cylindrical based granaries, as well as the areas of trapeziums, triangles, and truncated triangles. Many more astonishing mathematical calculations have been uncovered within the Great Pyramid:

> Mathematicians have detected in it the exact value of "pi", the exact average distance between the sun and the earth, the polar diameter of the earth, and so on.[16]

Egyptians perhaps initially established the science of geometry to measure and divide the land for growing crops; and to determine property boundaries after the flooding of the river. That geometry eventually contributed to the development of architectural mathematics and the construction of the pyramids and other monuments.

Astronomy

Similar, to mathematics, astronomy was an important tool which enabled Africans to adapt to their environment and to predict the behavior of the Nile and other bodies of water which the people depended on for survival.

Perhaps for that reason, or for reasons of shear curiosity, Africans of Nabta Playa in the Nubian Desert, began tracking the cycle of the star Sirius, between 12,000 BC and 11,000 BC. This led to the invention of the celestial stone Calendar Circle and observatory of Nabta Playa circa 6400 BC, and the invention of the lunar calendar in 4236 BC. These African astronomers, who constructed the Great

Pyramids and parts of the stone Calendar Circle in perfect alignment with the three stars of Orion's belt, are the reason that we are able today to make appointments in our daily, weekly, and monthly planners. Calendars are astronomical inventions.

The fact that this is so, reminds us of Copernicus, the renaissance astronomer whose research led to many modern scientific discoveries. One can only imagine where he would have begun had it not been for the knowledge of the African astronomers who invented the celestial and lunar calendars. One thing is for certain, had it not been for African astronomy, mathematics, and science in general, we would not have yet achieved the modern scientific advances that we are all familiar with, such as the computer or space shuttle; and it is probable that humanity would be behind in the advancement of scientific knowledge by thousands of years.

Music

James writes in stolen Legacy regarding the art of music, "Music (or Harmony) meant the living practice of philosophy i.e., the adjustment of human life into harmony with God..." Africans began to study the art of music thousands of years ago. Since music meant the adjustment of human life into harmony with God, then by definition, it is pleasant and perhaps healing. This is precisely the manner in which the high priests of Egypt used it. They discovered that the harmony in the music was therapeutic and therefore healing. Since that time, over the next thousands of years of practice, Africans have developed a unique and complex polyrhythmic musical harmony, based on those origins. For this reason, Africans developed unique forms of music including reggae, spirituals, gospel, blues, jazz; rhythm and blues and rock and roll. Singers such as Sarah Vaughn, Nina Simone, Stevie Wonder, Coltrane, Bob Marley, Gil Scott Heron, Miles Davis, Rachell Ferrell, Erika Badu, Jill Scott, Jennifer Hudson, Alicia Keys, Muddy Waters and Mahalia Jackson, among others, all embody, through their voices and instruments, the living practice of philosophy, or the adjustment of human life into harmony with God.

Writing and Documentation

During the Dark Ages Europe lost touch with the African arts and sciences. As a result, Europe fell back to the uncivilized state that existed prior to its contact with Africa. None of the knowledge, which was widely disseminated throughout Europe by the Greeks and Romans, was indigenous to Europe; hence, Europe relied, in part, upon hidden Greek and Latin manuscripts of African knowledge to spark the Renaissance. Once the Renaissance was well underway and cultural civilization had slowly returned, some learned Europeans asserted that Africans were incapable of developing their own written language!

Nubian Alphabet

Africans created the art of documentation and writing. Narmer's Palette contains the first written inscriptions. Although it is unclear, as to how early the date of the African inscriptions, Narmer's Palette itself dates to 4000 BC, the same time that Africans also wrote the *Book of the Dead*, which is the first book of spiritual salvation. Narmer's Palette also marks the point at which pre-history ends and the historic era began. Narmer, the Nubian who unified Upper and Lower Egypt, probably carried with him from Nubia the written characters used on Narmer's Palette.

The Nubians, like the Egyptians, used hieroglyphics to document and write their histories, however, around 500 BC, Nubia invented an alphabet, known as the Meroitic alphabet.

The Nubian's hieroglyphic written language, which they used during their common daily activities, was akin the Egyptian hieroglyphs. Yet, they soon developed a shorthand version for use in their business and trade affairs. The shorthand version, with fewer characters, was faster and more efficient than writing with full hieroglyphs. From that shorthand version, the Nubians eventually went on to invent their own alphabet from which, one could argue, sprung the Greek and Roman alphabets especially when considering the use of vowels, and the fact that Greece was once an Egyptian colony:

> ...the two scripts of the Meroitic language employ 23 characters that incorporate vowel notations. As a result, this Nubian language may be described as a syllabic system because every one of the 23 signs potentially represents a consonant plus a vowel, which in most cases is an A, except when followed by another symbol used to indicate the vowels I, O, and E... within this notational system there is a sign that serves not only as a divider between words but also separates, on occasion, grammatical elements...[17]

Obviously, not only were Africans first to document with a written language, they also produced an alphabet complete with vowels, consonants, and grammatical elements. Unfortunately, the Nubian alphabet has not yet been deciphered. Even more unfortunate, most of the Nubian antiquities and monuments have been flooded under water because of the damming of the Nile River by the Arabs in Egypt.

Nubia

Arabs migrated to Egypt in 640 AD. They did not build the monuments in Egypt or Nubia (Sudan) and have no claim to Egyptian or Nubian historical monuments. In fact, under Arab custodianship tourist visiting Egypt desecrated and trashed the African stone Calendar Circle, at Nabta Playa. Since the discovery of the site, vandals knocked over or rearranged the original megaliths from their standing position. This is what happens to African history when it is under the custodianship of others. The Arabs in Egypt also removed the limestone coverings off the outer surfaces of the Pyramids, to construct buildings in Cairo.

This occupation of African lands by Arabs is destructive on the monuments as well as the people. Genocide was committed in Darfur, and Arab aircraft attack defenseless, Nubian women, children, and elderly villagers in the Nuba Mountains of Sudan. These are the descendents of the great Nubian civilization. That Nubian civilization and the Egyptian civilization are well over 5,000 years old, perhaps closer to 10,000 years old; and most of its indigenous people have dispersed throughout the African continent. When media reports on the age of the Egyptian civilization, they are referring to the non-Arab, indigenous Egyptians, since Arabs did not enter Egypt until around 640 AD. The indigenous Egyptians, the Nubians, are Black and resemble the very first pharaoh Narmer (Menes).

If Arabs were to occupy China, of course, they would have no claim to China's ancient civilization. The ancient Egyptians were Africans, and Africans created the arts and sciences and built the monuments and Pyramids. Despite Josephus' fantasy of a Jewish antiquity, Jews did not exist during the construction of the Pyramids, and Arabs were nomadic shepherds in Asia.

Arabs have no true connection are affinity towards the Egyptian or Nubian cultural monuments. Perhaps this is the reason they built the first Aswan dam in the late nineteenth century to create a reservoir for irrigation purposes. This resulted in the submergence of the Nubian monuments for most times of the year. In 1960, Arabs built a second dam in Aswan to generate electricity for Egypt; the result was the displacement of thousands upon thousands of Nubians, and the loss of countless Nubian monuments and antiquities underwater.

This area of the Nile River was important because through the antiquities and monuments, one would plainly see the close cultural nexus between the ancient Egyptian and Nubian people. Perhaps among the artifacts submerged under water were ancient written manuscripts that could help decipher more about the Nubian culture and their relationship with Egypt. One can only wonder what Africans and humanity in general has lost forever. Today Nubians are demanding a return to their indigenous homelands in Egypt.

With the on-going campaign to marginalize and malign Africa's contribution to civilization, it is safe to assume that Arabs built the dams with indifference to the ancient Nubian artifacts and monuments. Because they could have built an electricity generating dam elsewhere to avoid the displacement of the Nubian people in the south, and the destruction of their ancient culture.

Fortunately, the United Nations undertook to save what monuments they could by relocating some to higher ground. Other monuments found homes in museums around the world, including the United States. All Africans should be concerned about the buried or submerged Nubian artifacts and monuments, because there is a connection between all Africans in the Diaspora and ancient Egyptian and Nubian civilizations.

Historical evidence demonstrates the migratory gene flow of the ancient Africans of the Great Lakes region and Nabta Playa, to the Nubians near the Nile and north into Egypt. Later, Africans would migrate out of Egypt and Nubia to the south, north and west parts of Africa, and across the Atlantic into North and South America.

So, any suggestion that Africans in the African Diaspora, including those located in the Americas, have no rightful claim to Egypt and Nubia, is simply untrue. All Africans in the Diaspora have a right to the legacy of both the Egyptian and Nubian civilizations, in the same way that Britain and all whites; for example, claim Greece and Rome as their progenitors. Although it appears that, the only connection the British had with ancient Rome was as slaves because Cicero, upon his return from a visit to Britain, admonished Julius Caesar to "not take the British as slaves, for they cannot be taught to dance." Caesar apparently took them anyway. So much for Britain's connection with Rome and its connection with Greece is equally remote. The fact is that Greece and Rome looked toward their Northern European neighbors with utmost disdain, due to their savagery.

All Africans in the African Diaspora have cultural ties to Nubia and Egypt; and most tribes of people throughout the African continent, including Egypt, point to Nubia as their birthplace. The intercontinental migration of the ancient Egyptian and Nubian Aten-monotheists, attest to this fact. The general population also migrated out of Egypt and Nubia, perhaps due to their frustration with the occupation of their land by white foreigners, intermittently, starting in 342 BC, and the abolition of their Mystery System by the Romans in later centuries.

The following quote from Diop is further proof of this nexus between ancient Egypt, Nubia and all Africans in the African Diaspora:

> ...Nubia appears to be closely akin to Egypt and the rest of Black Africa. It seems to be the starting point of both civilizations. So we are not astonished today to find many civilizing features common to Nubia, whose kingdom lasted until the British Occupation, and the remainder of Black Africa. Right after the end of the Egypt-Nubian Antiquity,

the Empire of Ghana soared like a meteor from the mouth of the Niger to the Senegal River, circa the third century A.D. Viewed in this perspective, African history proceeded without interruption. The first Nubian dynasties were prolonged by the Egyptian dynasties until the occupation of Egypt by the Indo-Europeans, starting in the fifth century BC. Nubia remained the sole source of culture and civilization until about the sixth century A.D., and then Ghana seized the torch from the sixth century until 1240, when its capital was destroyed by Sundiata Keita. This heralded the launching of the Mandingo empire (capital: Mali) ...Next came the empire of Gao, the empire of Yatenga (or Mossi, still in existence), the kingdoms of Djoloff and Cayor (in Senegal), destroyed by Faidherbe* under the Napoleon III. In listing this chronology, we have simply wanted to show that there was no interruption in African history. It is evident that, if starting from Nubia and Egypt, we had followed a continental geographical direction, such as Nubia-Gulf of Benin, Nubia-Congo, Nubia-Mozambique, the course of African history would still have appeared to be uninterrupted.[18]

9

A Tale of Two Continents
AD 300 to 1100 AD

The Greek and the Roman dispersion of African knowledge by way of war and trade, led to the development of other previously uncivilized parts of Europe. That development combined with a maritime expansion and discovery of gunpowder, would later afford Europe a decided advantage over Africa.

What was Europe like in between 12,000 BC and 10,000 BC, when African astronomers began to track the motion of celestial bodies? In 6400 BC, when the stone Calendar Circle and observatory was invented? In 4236 BC when Egypt invented the lunar Calendar? In 4000 BC, when the world's first writings were itched into Narmer's Palette and into the authorship of the first spiritual book of salvation? In 2600 BC, when the genius Imhotep constructed the world's first stone building, the step pyramid of Saqqara? What was Europe like in 2500 BC, during construction of the Great Pyramids, in exact alignment with the three stars of Orion's belt? The Africans also established the first institution of higher learning, which taught the first system of spiritual salvation known as the Egyptian Mystery System. Where was Europe when Africans developed grammar, rhetoric, an alphabet, logic, philosophy, geometry, arithmetic, astronomy, engineering, medicine, surgery, music, and religion?

Some European Egyptologists have left behind a sad legacy of manipulation, fabrication and deceit that belies all science. However, any scientist who allows his or her own bias to influence a scientific conclusion fails science. For the most part, Europeans approached the subject of Egyptology with a racist superiority complex. Nevertheless, while they attempt to nullify African achievements and contributions to civilization, they have nothing to say about ancient Europe. There is a reason for this odd behavior. During the time when African civilization was well underway, Europeans were uncivilized, to put it mildly; they could neither read nor write and perhaps worshiped oak trees or something similar.

The truth has strength that lies and deceit cannot stand up to. According to Greek tradition, the colonization of Greece happened around 1550 BC, by Cadmus the Phoenician and by the Egyptians, Danaus and his brother Aegptus. The Greeks learned writing and metallurgy at that time.[1] About eight hundred years later, Rome learned what it knew from Greece. Obviously, the African colonists, by virtue of their proximity to the Mediterranean introduced Rome and Greece to civilization. Once civilized, the Romans and Greeks looked upon the uncivilized Europeans to their North as blue-eyed savages. This was an accurate description as cannibalism was the norm, and men were the most dangerous predators in Europe at the time.[2] The Irish consumed their own fathers upon their deaths; for example, and had intercourse with their mothers and sisters.[3] Further, "as late as the twelfth century A.D., the kings of one Irish clan still celebrated their coronations by engaging in ritual sexual intercourse with a horse."[4]

What accounts for this type of behavior by Europeans? Diop explains it this way:

> The history of humanity will remain confused as long as we fail to distinguish between the two early cradles in which Nature fashioned the instincts, temperament, habits, and ethical concepts of the two subdivisions before they met each other after a long separation dating back to prehistoric times.

The first of the two cradles according to Diop was the Nile Valley:

> The abundance of the vital resources, its sedentary, agricultural character, the specific conditions of the valley, will engender in man, that is, in the [African], a gentle, idealistic, peaceful nature, endowed with a spirit of justice and gaiety.

Diop compares the Nile valley environment and conditions that shaped the peaceful demeanor and nature of Africans with the harsh environment in Europe and Eurasia:

> By contrast, the ferocity of the nature in the Eurasian steppes, the barrenness of those regions, the overall circumstances of material conditions, were to create instincts necessary for survival in such an environment. Here, Nature left no illusion of kindliness: it was implacable and permitted no negligence; man must obtain his bread by the sweat of his brow. Above all, in the course of a long, painful existence, he must learn to rely on himself alone, on his own possibilities. He could not indulge in the luxury of believing in a beneficent God who would shower down abundant means of gaining a livelihood; instead, he would conjure up deities maleficent and cruel, jealous and spiteful: Zeus, Yahweh, among others.

Thus, nature is responsible for the warlike predatory demeanor of Europeans and Indo-Europeans:

> All of the peoples of the area, whether white or yellow, were instinctively to love conquest, because of a desire to escape from those hostile surroundings. The milieu chased them away; they had to leave it or succumb, try to conquer a place in the sun in a more clement nature. Invasions would not cease, once an initial contact with the Black world to the south had taught them the existence of a land where the living was easy, riches abundant, technique flourishing. Thus, from 1450 B.C. until Hitler, from the Barbarians of the fourth and fifth centuries to Genghis Khan and the Turks, those invasions from east to west or from north to south continued uninterrupted.[5]

The Roman invasion into Africa, and subsequent theft of African knowledge was not enough. In 4th century AD, and again in the 6th century AD, Rome dealt a major blow by abolishing the Egyptian Mystery System, which was the source of Africa's religion, art, science, and philosophy. To Rome's benefit, the abolition enabled Christianity to grow and flourish in its place. To facilitate Rome's effort to control the masses of new Christian converts within its territories; Rome reseated the Coptic

Christian church from Africa to Rome.

Destruction of knowledge can never be a good thing, however, because ignorance in the face of it will dispel quickly. Therefore, the abolition of the Egyptian Mystery System by Rome, as it turns out, was a serious miscalculation for this reason. The African knowledge, which was now under the guardianship of Greece and Rome, was not intuitive, homegrown, or native to Europe. If the knowledge became lost; for example, would they be capable of recreating astronomy, engineering, medicine, surgery, philosophy, geometry, and architectural mathematics, which they learned from Africa? Evidently, the answer is no. After the fall of Rome in AD 476, knowledge did indeed abandon Europe. The effect of abolishing the Egyptian Mystery System, combined with the fall of Rome, propelled Europe into the same uncivilized state prior to their contact with Africa. That state, the European Dark Ages would last AD 476 to AD 1100. Nearly 700 years of savagery, barbarianism and ignorance fell upon them.

Ghana

In the meantime, circa AD 300 Ghana, an ancient West African trading empire began to emerge. It was in present day Mali near the Niger River. The Ghanaians established control over a key Sahara trade route in the city of Autoghast, which trade merchants passed through on their journey. In addition to the key trade route, Ghana controlled a large reserve of gold within its territory and was able to manipulate the market by monopolizing supply and demand; hence, they became very wealthy gold traders.

The use of the unruly camel as a source of transport was very important to Ghana. The camel unlike the horse or donkey could travel long distances without the need for water, thus allowed for the expansion of trade east and north across the Sahara. Caravans of camels carried copper, spices, ivory, salt, and gold to the northern tip of Africa, allowing them access to Egyptian, Greek and Roman markets. Rome and Greece, before the Dark Ages, required West African gold to make its coinage but there was also demand elsewhere for ornaments and jewelry. The Ghana kingdom became very wealthy as a result. That strong financial standing enabled them to call up a military of 200,000 men in a campaign to expand their territory. That expansion transformed Ghana from a kingdom into a powerful empire, with the annexing of several minor kingdoms and lucrative trade routes. Because of the annexation of the minor kingdoms, the king of Ghana was renamed Musa— the king of kings. The Ghana Empire is at that time a place of cultivated learning. In the later successor states of Mali and Songhai, books became prized possessions and gold was plentiful. The Ghana Empire began to decline circa 1,100 AD. That was right about the time when Europe slowly began to emerge from the Dark Ages, after nearly 700 years of uncivilized ignorance and barbarianism.

The Mandingo people established the successor empire of Mali ca 1,235 AD to ca 1,600 AD. Mali became a constitutional monarchy with laws and customs that were the envy of many. Those Africans established the first university in the world as a center of learning at Timbuktu, although Egyptians established the first institution of higher learning at Annu (ON) Egypt, thousands of years prior. This is the state of Mali during the reign of Mansa Musa, AD 1,307 to 1,332 AD:

> The wealth of the kingdom, the splendor of the court and administrative behavior were known as well in Europe as in Cairo.[6]

The Mandingo people were also accomplished sailors, apparently reaching the New World before Columbus:

> The ships of Mali are said to have reached the Canary Islands off the northwestern coast of Africa. In 1310 Abubakari II, heading 2000 ships sailed out the Senegal River to the Atlantic Ocean and to the New World. This was one hundred and eighty-one years before Columbus. The Mandingos of Mali were the ancestors of the fictionalized Kunta Kinte who, four centuries later, was enslaved and taken to

America in chains.[7]

Some 700 years before European slavery, the African Moors of North Africa combined with Africans from Senegal to the southwest of them and formed "the most powerful military machines the world had ever seen." This powerful combination of African and African Moorish soldiers invaded Spain, France, and Rome:

> For the first time in recorded history, a non-white people were dominant in Europe. As conquerors have done since time began, the Africans began and enormous traffic in slaves... From far away Holland, Sweden and Finland, slaves were brought. The trade reached out to Greece and southern Russia... Thousands of Spaniards were sold into slavery in Africa and the Middle East.[8]

It is evident that the African-Moorish invasion had a civilizing effect on Europe, because the African-Moorish tandem was safekeeping the knowledge of the Mystery System. The Wolof people of Senegal are descendants of the ancient Egyptians, while the Moors descended from Carthage, which was an ancient colony of Egypt. The Egyptians passed to them, many secrets of the Mystery System, including mathematical theory. With the return of the Mystery System knowledge, Europe is able to evolve out of the Dark Ages.

The European Dark Ages lasted some 700 years, but in the 15th century, 300 years after the Dark Ages, Europe would embark upon a maritime revolution that enabled it to expand its trade and gain access to new commodities such as gunpowder. The gunpowder, evidently, would change the course of history.

The maritime expansion in Europe came through European sailing excursions up and down the west coast of Africa. Around circa AD 1500 the European slave trade officially began when the Portuguese ventured onto the African continent, and crossed the Senegal River. This is where they began their trade in gold and enslaved Africans, which brought them very much wealth. Because of the lucrative trade, they became motivated to obtain more gold and unfortunately, more enslaved Africans. The new found wealth, in turn allowed them to create some important maritime innovations—most notably the compass. The compass enabled Europeans to navigate the seas more accurately and over longer distances to places such as India and China. China, around the 15th century, was the place where Europeans discovered for themselves the explosive nature of gunpowder.

Ancient Egyptians used gunpowder for ceremony. Later, the Chinese used gunpowder in both ceremony and weaponry. Yet the explosive combination of saltpeter, sulfur,and charcoal, in the hands of the European, would change the course of history. It could not have come at a worse time for

Africa or the rest of the world. After nearly a thousand years of barbarianism and degradation, in the late 15th century, Europe would emerge with a renewed fervor to exploit the natural resources and wealth of foreign lands.

The invention of the canon came almost immediately after Europe obtained gunpowder. The assembly of canons on the merchant ships became a great advantage at sea. With the assembly of canons into smaller musket rifles, Europe gained an equal military advantage on land. Europeans used the canon and the musket to conquer and colonize Africans and others throughout the world.

The Xhosa and Zulu of Southern Africa would soon encounter the SLC24A5 type who reached the tip of South Africa by ship. The whites, Xhosa and Zulu Africans would eventually engage in many battles over the control of African land. The whites believed in private land ownership; however, Africans had no concept of such a thing. They believed the land belonged to everybody just like the sun.

The Xhosa and Zulu, with spears, swords, and military precision, defeated the whites and their musket rifles soundly. Because of the defeat, whites believed the Africans possessed magical powers, as they would not die from gunfire. The war for the whites was not lost, however. Finally, after many hard-fought battles by Africans to hold onto their land, Europeans would soon return with many more men and guns. Africans did not stand a chance against the superior fire power of the musket rifle; thousands of them died by European gunfire. The magic of the Xhosa and Zulu was not magic at all; it was simply the inaccurate trajectory of the musket rifle.

With the defeat of the Xhosa and Zulu warriors, the SLC24A5 type set its sights northward, with intent on conquering the entire African continent. Nature would stop them in their tracks. The tropical zones north of South Africa were home to many deadly diseases such as malaria and others. The whites began to die off, and retreated to the southern tip of Africa where they would eventually set up and impose the wicked system of Apartheid. Nature is what prevented the whites from occupying the entire African continent with their guns and canons. Unfortunately, nature could not prevent the Trans-Atlantic slave trade, colonialism, or neo-colonialism. All those systems caused Africa to regress into their own dark ages, from which it has yet to emerge.

10

On Race and Status

The ancient Egyptians were in constant contact with their Nubian neighbors. Exchange of culture, trade and marriage between the neighbors was commonplace. They were both African people, of course, but Nubians founded the first dynasty in Egypt and were the Kings and Queens of many Egyptian dynasties. As described by Herodotus, ancient Egyptians were the progeny of the Nubians; this is affirmed by studies that demonstrate a south to north genetic flow of peoples through the Nile valley. Later, Egypt also encountered foreigners who were white or Semitic types, and would consequently categorize the foreigners they encountered based on their experiences with them. Within that categorization, the Egyptians established a hierarchy of humans.

The Egyptians ranked themselves and their

Nubian neighbors on the top of the human hierarchy; while Sea people and foreigners from the east including Semites and whites, were ranked at the bottom. One can find this hierarchy of people according to color on bas-reliefs throughout Egypt. From front to back, depictions of each type were as follows: Egyptian-Nubian-Semitic-white— the further the position to the rear, the lower the ranking. The rankings always followed this pattern because the Egyptians generally viewed whites and Semites negatively. The basis of the negative ranking was the result of the Egyptian repeated encounters with them, rather than skin color. As mentioned earlier, the Egyptians and Nubians had the utmost distain for the wondering shepherds of Asia and Indo-Europe because they continually encroached upon African territory.

Around the 6th century BC, the marauding white people and Indo-Europeans repeatedly attempted to pillage and plunder Egypt without success. Despite this fact, whites, at the time, did not harbor a visceral hatred toward the Egyptians because they were Black. Although the whites were quite aware of their white skin and of the Egyptian's black skin, it was not the reason for their repeated attempts to topple the Egyptian civilization. Simply put, the whites invaded because the settled, Black Africans had what they did not have—civilization and wealth. This was the case described in the biblical allegory of Cain and Abel—where, at some point in time, roaming shepherds eventually encroached upon the settled agriculturally based people and their lands. Again, this biblical allegory was probably in reference to the invasion and occupation of the nomadic Hyksos shepherds of Asia into Egypt. This is why the Egyptians had such a strong disliking for nomads and shepherds, and such was the case with the invading white people. The white people were not the only ones who wanted what the Egyptians possessed. Envy of the Egyptian civilization and material wealth was the reason for all the attempted invasions by foreigners; unfortunately, for the whites, they were defeated, captured, and held as slaves. This is how the white SLC24A5 gene types first returned to Africa after about a 10,000year absence; they were defeated and held in Egypt, as captured slaves. This tendency to invade and encroach upon the land is the reason Egyptians viewed Asian, Semitic, and white shepherds as primitive, destructive, pillagers; hence, their placement on the lower rungs of the Egyptian human hierarchy.

Today, we have a modern more sinister hierarchy of man based upon the false concept of *race*. The false concept of *race*, as we know it today, most likely evolved around the time of the Trans-Atlantic enslavement of Africans. However, it did not begin with whites espousing a venomous, racist hatred toward Africans. This would take place later, when it was necessary to justify the peculiar institution of slavery and to rationalize slavery on religious and moral grounds.

There was a practice among enemy African tribes to use captured prisoners as indentured servants. In the African practice, the treatment of indentured servants was relatively gentle, almost like that of any other member of a particular family or village. African indentured servitude was in no way comparable to the chattel type of slavery that the Europeans would administer. Eventually rival African tribes would exchange the prisoner-indentured-servants for European commodities such as guns and gun powder. The Europeans exploited this practice by instigating friction between the tribes and inciting them to war. This age-old European practice of divide and conquer assured a ready supply of captured Africans to enslave. But this was not a trade at all from the African perspective. It was the start of a chattel *race* war between color producing black people and the non-color producing SLC24A5 white-skin people around the world. This chattel race war is global and perpetual.

Enslaved Africans would literally work to death, so the demand for new slaves steadily increased. The high death rate, as a result, was not an added expense to the plantation owners because insurance companies provided policies on the lives of each slave. For this reason, the incentive was not to treat the enslaved Africans well, but literally work them to death. It was expensive, however, to replace and ship the human cargo. Consequently, each time a ship returned, like sardines in a can, Africans were packed:

> ...with as little as one square foot of sitting space, and generally chained by their necks and legs. They would remain in those positions, unable to move, over two week duration of the voyage.[1]

The cruelty of this only foreshadowed the treatment that awaited them on the plantations. What the African traders failed to realize was that the European and American type chattel slavery would have no resemblance to the indentured servitude which they knew of; but would become the most cruel and oppressive form of slavery ever known to mankind. It consisted of savage tactics, such as lynching, burnings, castration, and rape, which served to terrorize African people. Therefore, it was necessary for white slavers to rationalize such behavior:

> There was also a moral degradation: of the slaves, and of the slavers. Through enslaving Africans, Europeans abused their own humanity as well. He came to believe that Africa was indeed cast away in savage chaos, that Africans had never known any reasonable social order of their own, and that African slaves deserved no better than they got. The slavers justified their work by such beliefs.[2]

Justify they did. The slave trade was miserably cruel but lucrative, so whites began to demonize Africans and label them as sub-human, savage, uncivilized, etc. This rationalization is necessary at the time, because the free slave labor brought unimaginable riches to the white plantation owners in Europe as well as North and South America.

Flavius Josephus and others first planted the seeds of discontent in the first century A.D. Then, Josephus and his ilk bantered about the idea of the so-called differences among men and the idea of who were the chosen people of God. By the 18th and 19th centuries, during the fertile era of the Trans-Atlantic slave trade, (war) those seeds of discontent would germinate and grow into the false concept of *race* and the ideology of racism:

> Up to the 1770s or so, the Americas as a whole received more Africans by way of the slave trade than its total number of immigrants from Europe. Especially in Brazil, the Caribbean, and the southern American colonies, Africans were known only as slaves. In these societies, and ultimately in Europe as well, [African] skin color, hair texture, and facial features were associated with the status of slavery. Prejudice based on culture and that based on social rank were blended together and expressed as a "racial" prejudice.[3]

Concept of Race

With that, we have finally come to the practical details. The seeds of discontent and general animosity have finally germinated and blossomed into this concept of *race*. This is where the one tenth of one percent difference among men, such as skin color, hair texture and physical features became tools to negatively categorize and classify humans without the knowledge of their true history and culture. It is by no coincidence that this animosity grew as Europe's plantations brought in more and more profit from the free African labor:

> As the Industrial revolution progressed into the nineteenth century, Europeans found their technological superiority increasing rapidly....Europeans were now creating the first industrialized society the world had known. Few people are capable of viewing the world over the long perspective of time, and it was easy to equate technological expertise with a general superiority of Europeans over all other peoples.[4]

Although preserved for all to see, Europeans would ignore, omit, manipulate, conceal or lie about African civilization, which through its arts and science laid the groundwork for future world technological advances. Instead, there is a wholesale marginalization and maligning of African people throughout the world, which continues to this day.

It should be clear now, as to why Europeans have attempted to classify Nubians and Egyptians as something other than Black Africans and why factual African history will never be taught. To sell white supremacy, they must convince Africans that their ancestors came out of the trees and contributed nothing to world civilization. That the people who built the ancient civilizations of Nubia and Egypt were white, or something other than African; and all the historical characters of the Old Testament were also white, including Moses and his sister Miriam. This is the kind of delusion associated with racism, and why it is considered a mental disorder.

In the eighteenth and nineteenth centuries, the false concept of *race* would be watered and fertilized with the best manure that biological and social scientists could muster up. Scientists would eventually categorize the *races* into four colors: black, red, yellow and white. With this categorization, coupled with the arrogance of the Europeans based on their industrial success, came the ranking of men.

There was no consideration at all given to the role of the institution of slavery and its negative impact on Africa's development. Africans were on the bottom rung of human ranking, and as can be expected given their historical amnesia, Europeans placed themselves at the top.

The reader may recall that Egyptians ranked

whites at the bottom rung of the human hierarchy, and studied astronomy before the existence of Mesopotamia. In addition, a lethal military machine consisting of soldiers from North and West Africa conquered and enslaved Europe in the 8th century. Yet in the early nineteenth century, Europeans claimed that Mesopotamian civilization pre-dated Nubian and Egyptian civilizations:

> Historians of this period were also busy working out the comparative histories which were to culminate in the works of Spengler and Toynbee. The claim was made by most that the "human race" developed in Mesopotamia and stayed there until after the flood, after which it moved out. Civilization went northwest. The Africans, such historians either said or implied, obviously had taken another direction.[5]

The reader may recall that Josephus also argued that Abraham introduced astronomy into Egypt. Yet, we know this to be false because of the evidence, which demonstrates that circa 12,000BC; Africans began to track the movement of the stars. These same Africans in ca 6400 BC built an astronomical stone Calendar Circle and observatory from which they tracked the celestial skies and recorded data for thousands of years. In addition, at the time of the invention of the celestial and lunar calendars, by the Egyptians in 4236 BC, Mesopotamia had not yet come into existence.

Also, we know today that the first women, the Mitochondrial Eves was not just one woman but a group of closely related women who lived in the Makgadikgadi basin (Kalahari Desert) and is the most recent common ancestor of all human kind. Every living human today, can trace his or her DNA back to the African Mitochondrial Eve. Hence, it was from Africa that humanity sprung forth to populate the entire world.

Above is just one example of what revisionist European historians wrote in the eighteenth and early nineteenth centuries with the claim that humanity developed in Mesopotamia. The African astronomers of Nabta Playa, the Mitochondrial Eve, and the SLC24A5 mutated gene, are, in this case, historical truths that prevail over the ignorance and deception of revisionists.

Now the table has been set. The concept of *race* is fully blossomed. Institutions, to influence policy making, exploit the individual prejudice, animosity, ignorance, and general feeling of superiority among everyday individual white people. The policies can assure that whites obtain and hold on to economic, political, and judicial power at the expense of people of color. This is the ideology of racism. Again, racism has to do with the relative power between *races* of people; in its initial conceptualization, it means the relative power between white and African (Black) people.

Although institutions such as government and

corporations impose racism, it could not be successful without the white-supremacy mindset of the average, everyday white individual. Within the white supremacy mindset, lurks an innate and visceral discomfort and extreme disliking toward people of African descent, and all people of color.

This mindset is shared by white conservatives and liberals alike, and it goes something like this: economic, educational, and judicial discrimination are justified because the underlying assumption is that people of African descent are lazy, unintelligent, criminally inclined, and generally inferior; hence, are not capable of working hard, of scholastic achievement or adhering to societies laws.

The Ideology of Racism

With the white supremacy mindset in the backdrop, governments developed laws to force the false notion of inferiority upon Black people, such as Apartheid and Jim Crow Segregation. More recent policy making, such as that which took place under Reaganomics, accomplished the same end as Apartheid and Jim Crow:

> The most dramatic legacy of the Reagan era has been its institutionalization of his brand of conservatism, in which the remnants of the New Deal and welfare [state-ism] were replaced with free-market economics,

government deregulation of business, and the abandonment of attempts to promote social equality or to guarantee adequate provision of employment, housing, nutrition, health care, education, or income. The administration's argument was that egalitarianism and redistribution of wealth led to a static, even depressed, economy. Inequality was a requisite result of sound economic growth, and the wealth created by the rich would lift up the poor as well, by way of a "trickle down." By the end of the 1980's, Social Darwinism was the accepted theory in Washington.[6]

This trickle-down theory further widened the gap between the wealthy and the poor in the United States. The poor Americans who are victims of Reaganomics include African-Americans as well as white Americans. Yet, because of American *race* politics, impoverished and working-class white Americans will generally vote for policies such as Reaganomics, which go against their own best interests.

Race politics, therefore, is an old standby for white politicians, who seek to keep underclass whites and people of color in America from forming coalitions for common grievances. Groups and individuals, who overtly espouse racial hatred, are indirectly beneficial to politicians who seek to play *race* politics. It is obvious that both liberals and conservatives play *race* politics very well, when needed.

In agreement with Reagan's neo-conservatism, excluding the neo-conservative policy toward Israel, are fringe groups such as the neo-Nazis and Ku Klux Klan. Conservatives consider them extreme, and on the fringe; thus, generally do not welcome them among their ranks. This is so because hate groups tend not to play the political correctness game, and are thus more honest about voicing their politics.

Take David Duke as an example. He is a Klansman with an extreme admiration for all things related to Hitler and the Nazis. Unlike the average member of the Klan, he was articulate, well-dressed, youthful, and generally presentable in a media setting. He campaigned for Louisiana's sixth congressional district, voicing his opposition to,

> ...Busing, gun control, taxes, criminals, discrimination against white people, and all that regulation and interference from Washington.[7]

The reason his campaign may sound familiar is that his political platform is the same as Reagan's or any republican candidate, for that matter. So why did many members of the Republican Party voice their opposition to David Duke at the time of his campaign? Because for political parties, democrat, and republican alike, the use of the word "nigger" is taboo, at least in a public setting. The Klansman David Duke, however, as a card-carrying member, was fond of using the epithet, both in public and private.

In today's politics, the actual utterance of the word is unnecessary, because policy and legislation can speak for itself. Of course, there are slip ups every now and then, but for the most part, today's politicians follow the script very well. It is a subtle thing. The general viewpoint is that racism is finished in America, with no place for debate in today's politics. According to both liberal and conservative media, an allegation of racism is simply playing the so-called *race* card. Yet, racism in America is alive and well. Like dirt, it hides under the proverbial carpet, waiting for politicians to make use of it at the beneficial time, in their *race* politics campaigns.

In 1958, George Wallace ran for Governor against an opponent, John Patterson, who had the support of the Klan. Wallace, seeking to take advantage of Patterson's strange bedfellows, hit the campaign trail. He put a bed on the back of a flatbed truck—asking the voters if his opponent, Patterson, was, "in bed with the Ku Klux Klan". This strategy of Wallace did not work, because Patterson won:

> ...and rewarded United Klan Wizard Robert Shelton with the state automobile tire contract. Wallace resolved not to be "outniggered" again and made friends with

the Klan.[8]

Hate groups speak and act in ways that polished conservative and liberal politicians never will. However, the words, and even the deeds, of hate groups such as the Klan, can prep undereducated, working class or poor white voters to vote for policies, against their own best interests. Thus, you have *race* politics. The subtle nurturing of the white racist mindset, particularly of the poor white underclass, and more broadly of all whites, conservative and liberal alike, by hate groups, radio shock jocks and conservative TV hosts, keeps *race* politics alive and well.

Today, a politician who, like Wallace, refuses to be "outniggered" only has to utilize his inventory of clever, subtle code-words to stir to frenzy, the emotions of the average white voter. To drive this point home, the means and methods may have changed somewhat, but the Klan has been for over one hundred years:

> ...a secret, terrorist society dedicated to maintaining white rule in the United States.[9]

Between 1956 and 1962, there were seventy-five terrorist bombings of mostly African American targets, including a church, causing the death of four young girls. The outrage from that act precipitated a government crack-down on the Klan organization. As a result, in the 1970's, membership in the Klan declined; however, around 1980, it had a resurgence, and not coincidentally, during the Reagan neo-conservative movement. A polished, articulate racist such as David Duke linked together the terrorist Klan and the politics of the republican conservative right wing— different means and methods to reach the same end.

Insecurity and Contempt

The strong are generally tolerant, but insecurity can breed within a person, contempt toward others. This is a bit of human nature that many of us already know intuitively. We all learn as children that bullies have this kind of insecurity or self-loathing. Because a star football player on campus who gets failing grades; for example, may bully a nerd because the nerd has brains. What the bully hates about himself is the fact that he is not very smart in the classroom; and that breeds within him, contempt toward the scholar. He wants what the scholar has—brains.

Now, what could be behind the contempt or extreme disliking toward a group of people simply based on a physical characteristic, such as skin color? We know; for example, that whites in general, harbored an extreme hatred toward African Americans simply by the nature of the American pogrom. These organized American killings were entertainment events which entire white families attended, including children. White families commonly received hand bills advertising the next so called "nigger roast" to attend. A picnic of sorts, white families brought brown bag lunches to the festive atmosphere, and stared with amusement at the burning, lynching, whipping and castration of African American men.

Historical photos depict white parents smiling and pointing with their children at the dead African American men. This is a peculiar type of hate. A hatred that is rarely present among humans. What could be the catalyst that drives such extreme hate? In the *Isis Papers*, Frances Cress Welsing states,

> Acutely aware of their inferior genetic ability to produce skin color, whites built the elaborate myth of white genetic superiority. Furthermore, whites set about the huge task of evolving a social, political, and economic structure that would support the myth of the inferiority of Blacks and other non-whites.

It should now be apparent that the basis of the hatred, the catalyst that drives the ideology of racism, relates to the white conscious or subconscious awareness of the SLC24A5, genetic mutation. This awareness transforms into a visceral, innate, fundamental fear and peculiar hatred of some whites toward people of color and African people, in particular.

The awareness in some sense, of the SLC24A5 genetic mutation, binds them together in a confederacy or crusade against what they perceive to be a common threat or enemy. What is that common threat? Any self-described racist will tell you without hesitation, that white people face a threat of extinction.

This is what Hitler feared when he mistook the white Khazar converts to Judaism, as Semitics. He perceived them to be of mixed blood and wanted to keep his so called "superior" blood of white people pure. What he really feared was what he observed when people of color mixed with whites—the recessive nature of the white SLC24A5 gene causes it to dilute with color and disappear. This dominance, genetically speaking, of African blood over the recessive nature of white blood along with low birth rates, is the reason racists warn of the possible extinction of whites.

Hitler, in his quest to uncover a mythical beginning of his white so-called Aryan "master race" instructed German archaeologist not to dig so deep in Germany. Because Neanderthal Valley is in Western Germany, where evidence of Neanderthal man exits. Obviously, Hitler did not want archaeologists to uncover the bones of the Neanderthal man. For this reason, Hitler wanted to search somewhere outside of Germany, for the mythical birthplace of the white so-called Aryan. However, the following bit of information may cause Hitler to turn over in his grave. As mentioned above, in the 7 May 2010 issue of *Science* magazine, researchers from the Max-Planck Institute for

Evolutionary Anthropology in Germany published interesting data uncovering Neanderthal DNA in the genomes of modern-day Europeans and other non-Africans.[10]

The obvious irony of Hitler's quest to locate a birthplace for his white so-called "master race" is that, regardless of wherever on earth he had found them, if they were white, they were certain to carry Neanderthal DNA, along with the SLC24A5 skin-whitening gene mutation.

This means that Hitler's white, so-called "master race" are, according to today's science, not only part Neanderthal, but also mutants of the original people, African people. Suddenly, Neanderthal — the brutish, cannibalistic, cave dwelling dumbass is undergoing a reputational makeover by his progeny—interesting, but a challenging task for the most adept revisionists among them.

The recessive nature of the SLC24A5 gene versus the dominant nature of the African's reproductive genes is what Hitler feared. Genocide on the one hand, and the need for separation from the perceived threat on the other, are manifestations of this fear. Apartheid, Jim Crow segregation, anti-miscegenation, and white flight are some examples of this need for separation. In general, a racist such as David Duke believes that the increased numbers of non-white immigrants into the United States combined with the low birthrates of whites,

...Will make white people a minority totally

> vulnerable to the political, social, and economic will of [Blacks], Mexicans, Puerto Ricans, and Orientals.

He believed the solution to this so-called problem, is to separate the races:

> The Jews, [Blacks], Hispanics and Orientals would each be given a portion of the present-day United States so they could have a nation of their own. The rest of America would be reserved for the white majority.[11]

A flyer distributed by the Aryan Nations in 1981 is an example of the same fear of whites becoming extinct:

> The Death of the White Race...U.S. Commissioner confirms that white people face extinction

The caption below, placed under the photo of an interracial couple,

> "The Ultimate Abomination"[12]

It appears that the hate and insecurity of some whites, concerns the possibility of becoming extinct through interbreeding. Apartheid, segregation, and anti-miscegenation laws did exist for just that purpose. Rather than assimilate, it seems that some whites were more comfortable being isolated among themselves. What would happen however, if instead of separating, a sincere effort was undertook to bring white Americans and people of color together? The government could outlaw the confederate flag, and in the spirit of truth and reconciliation, make mandatory, the teaching of authentic African history to all children. Would this not obliterate the racist mindset over time, in the same way the hatred of white-Jews in America has apparently subsided?

The hatred of Jews in America was fervent until the neo-conservatives led by Reagan reversed their policy toward Israel. The media followed the neo-conservative line, and shaped the opinion of the public's view to a more positive one regarding the American white Jews. Thus, the government along with the media has important roles to play if there is to be a positive transformation of the racist mindset in America. Is goodwill between the *races* something that white people desire, given the recessive natural of the SLC24A5 gene? If true goodwill means that whites are free to mix and to procreate with people of color throughout the world, what would be the consequences of that?

11

African Influence in America

The African contribution to America has been great, in quality and quantity. African American soldiers have fought in every American war including the Revolutionary and Civil wars. Despite enslavement, terrorization, persecution and oppression in America, African American soldiers are loyal and valiant. African Americans have worked through politics, boycotts and civil disobedience, to ensure the Constitution works for everyone equally. African Americans have participated in political elected office ever since the Declaration of Independence. Unlike the so-called *model minority*, African Americans have never sat around on the sidelines waiting to reap the benefits garnered because of the struggles of others. In spite of racism and oppression, African Americans have always worked to improve America and the Constitution; and therefore, are patriots of the Constitution and model citizens.

The African American contribution included more than just free agricultural labor, in fact, without the African influence; America would not be as rich economically or culturally. We will demonstrate below; for example, that the Bantu language, unbeknownst to many, is a part of the American Southern English lexicon. The following quote further describes the African contribution:

> The history of the Americas would have been a very different one without the great contribution made by African labor, African arts, and African skills. The African's role in the growth of the sugar and tobacco plantations of the Caribbean and North America is well known. Less familiar is the African contribution in other fields. At least, until the early 19th century, the mines of Brazil were mainly worked by Africans who had learned their skills at home. The [Africans] also lent something of the traditional African style to the American crafts in which they engaged, and they engaged in many ...working as carpenters, masons, pavers, printers, sign and ornamental painters, carriage and cabinet makers, fabricators of military ornaments, lamp-makers, silversmiths, jewelers, and lithographers. If the slaves made many

things that Africa had never known, they nevertheless created them with the artistry and skill that derived from their native culture.[1]

Africans built much of the United States Capitol at Washington D.C. Those Africans, without any formal education in America, must have brought with them from Africa, craftsmanship along with artistic, scientific, and creative knowledge such as masonry, carpentry, and ironwork. That technical know-how, culture, and wisdom of Africans before they arrived in America is further evidenced by the useful, myriad inventions they created–especially during and immediately after the slavery period.

An interesting African contribution to America is the Bantu language itself. Bantu words in the American Southern English lexicon are relatively unknown, however. This is because many people assume that the Bantu words are of Native American origin. Before the arrival of Bantu in America, it was a common thread of language in Africa. This phenomenon further demonstrates the east to west migration of Africans across the African continent and across the Atlantic Ocean to the Americas. This is not mere speculation that a linguistic and cultural migration took place. The language of Senegal; for example, which is located on the west coast of Africa, have similarities with the language of the ancient Egyptians who of course, were in the northeast of the African continent.

<u>Egypt</u>
Atoum
Sek-met
Keti
Kaba
Antef
Fari: the Pharaoh
Meri, Meri
Ba-Ra
Ramses
Bakari

<u>Senegal</u>
Atu
Sek
Keti
Kaba, keba, kebe
Anta
Fari: title of emperor
Meri, Meri
Bara, Bari (Peul)
Reama, Rama
Bakari

In addition, the Yoruba who are a West African people located mostly in Nigeria share these common words with the Egyptian language:

Ran: name
Bu: place name
Amon: concealed
Miri: water
Ha: large house
Hor: to be high
Fahaka: silvery fish
Naprit: grain (or seed)

The Yoruba also knew of the following gods of Egypt:
Osiris, Isis, Horus, Shu, and sut, Thoth, Khepara, Amon, Anu, Khonsu, Khnum, Khopri, Hathor, Sokaris, Ra and Seb. The Yoruba people also made extensive use of hieroglyphics.
(Diop, *The African Origin of Civilization*, 182-186)

The Wolof tribes are a West African people located in Senegal, Gambia, and Mauritania. The following demonstrates that by simply replacing one letter (L replaces N or H replaces D) of an Egyptian word, the word translates into Wolof:

<u>Egyptian</u>
Nad: to ask
Nebt: braid, to braid
Ben-ben: source, spring
Nah: to protect, hide
Funa: sure, regular, authentic

<u>Wolof</u>
Lad: to ask
Let: braid, to braid
Bel-bel: to spring
Lah: to protect, hide
Fula: worthy, regular conduct
(Diop, *The African Origin of Civilization*, 155)

In addition to the above linguistic similarities between the ancient Egyptians and western Africans, there are also common cultural, artistic, spiritual, and philosophical practices and traditions. The abundance of these common practices among Africans could help to start an African renaissance:

> The oneness of the Egyptian and Black culture could not be stated more clearly. Because of this essential identity of genius, culture, and race, today all [Black Africans] can legitimately trace their culture to ancient Egypt and build a modern culture on that foundation. A dynamic, modern contact with Egyptian Antiquity would enable Blacks to

discover increasingly each day the intimate relationship between all Blacks of the continent and the mother Nile Valley. By this dynamic contact, the [African] will be convinced that these temples, these forests of columns, these pyramids, these colossi, these bas-reliefs, mathematics, medicine, and all this science, are indeed the work of his ancestors, and that he has a right and a duty to claim this heritage.[1]

Bantu in America

The linguistic similarities demonstrate that the cultural connection continued across the continent and across the Atlantic, to the Americas. Africans brought the Bantu language to America. As a result, Bantu words are part of the southern United States lexicon. The term Bantu itself means, the men:

> ...The stem Ntu of Bantu occurs in Wolof: Nit= man; and in Egyptian: Nti=man, someone; in Peul: Neddo= man. This designation of people by a generic term meaning man has been general throughout black Africa, starting with Egypt.[2]

The Trans-Atlantic slave trade displaced thousands upon thousands of Africans to the Caribbean, North America, and South America. The result was devastating to the culture and tradition of

African people. Yet, even cut off from their past, not all was lost or forgotten. Immersed into a foreign culture without the benefit of a formal education or knowledge of English, Africans adapted to their new environment with ingenuity:

> The problem of culture transference that faced the African slave in his new setting in the United States called forth every reserve of initiative and response, not only to adapt but also to survive. Given even the slightest similarity of situation with his African past, the slave came through with amazing aptitudes. The stately plantation homes throughout the south attest to this, with their graceful iron grillwork wrought by slaves who inherited a knowledge of metal work in from their ancestors, with their sweeping staircases and delicate entry ways made by black carpenters whose hands had carved designs in wood in the African forest. The kitchens of the south owe their famous southern recipes, known today around the world, to black cooks at work over the coals. The wide fields of cotton, rice, sugar, and indigo owe their great productivity to the same agricultural know-how that domesticated from wild plants the yam, the watermelon, cowpeas, okra, and palm and cola nuts. The basketwork of the Gullah [Blacks] is strikingly similar to the basketry

of the Congo, representing an artistic aptitude that crossed with the middle passage. Add to these similar situations the enjoyment of music, fireside tale-telling, and the communal dance and it will be seen that the slave readily adapted to new forms many skills and aptitudes from the past.[3]

As we shall see, later, those same skill sets and aptitudes also enabled the Africans to invent mechanisms and products that contributed to the industrial revolution, which was taking place during the 18th and 19th centuries. The Africans were ingenious inventors of a myriad of products during and after slavery, without the benefit of being formally educated—but with the skill set and expertise from their African past. Some of these inventions by African Americans are in the Appendices of this book.

Given the African's high aptitude and ability to adapt to their new environment, they met the challenge to communicate in an English-speaking society. Planters attempted to interact with the enslaved Africans on the plantations with their own English language; at the same time, discourage them from communicating with one another. The planters discouraged communication because they feared the possibility of insurrection. Therefore, they made sure that Africans for the most part, did not speak the same languages on any given plantation. What the slave traders did not realize, however, was that many of the captured Africans were from Bantu speaking regions, which covered a large expanse of African territory. Africans from diverse locations, spoke Bantu languages: Zulu-Bantu, Kiswahili-Bantu, Shona-Bantu, etc., but shared common Bantu words:

> ...the Bantu language group is spoken throughout most of Africa south of a line from the Cameroon to Kenya, that is, through the whole southern sub-continent. The Bantu speaking peoples are generally regarded as having come from the north; from the edge of the Sudan [Nubia]....The fact that Bantu languages are closely related to one another suggests that the separation from a parent language cannot have taken place more than about three millennia ago.[4]

The real Garden of Eden, the birthplace of Mitochondrial Eve is found in the Makgadikgadi basin in what is now modern-day Botswana. Eventually there were settlements in the Nile Valley, where the first human civilization developed. Much later, after repeated invasions and encroachments by foreigners, there was a migration from the Nile Valley (Egypt, Nubia) to the southeast, as well as to the central, north, and western parts of the African continent.

Slave traders assumed the languages spoken over this wide expanse of Africa were distinct. They were mistaken as mentioned, because many spoke Bantu languages, and could communicate with each other, using common Bantu words. The following are Bantu based languages and their regions: Central: Kongo, Lwena, Luba-Kasai and Luba-Katanga. East: Bemba, ILA, Rundi, and Swahili. South: Nyana and Yao, Shona, Uenda, Sotho, Zulu, and Kamba. North: teke, Tetela, Bobangi, Bulu, and Ruala.[5]

These diverse Bantu speaking Africans settled on different plantations throughout the Southern states. This fact made it possible for the Bantu language to become a part of the American English lexicon, particularly in the Southern states. Although confined on plantations the language imprints itself upon the wider Southern English lexicon, spoken by whites in the general population:

> The variety of African language groups and conditions of slavery were such that it was difficult for any particular African word to survive over a large area through its use by slaves alone. But here and there, planters would observe certain native words used by a few individuals to designate well-known objects like terrapins, peanuts, etc., and they would take up these words in their conversations with slaves. Then finding that other planters had encountered similar

words, they began to use the best-known ones in everyday speech and writing, thus giving them a sound basis for survival.[6]

Bantu words became place names in seven southern states. Some of the Bantu place names are similar in different states because as explained above, Africans spoke Bantu based languages from a wide swath of the African continent. Although they may have originated from diverse tribes and settled in diverse states via the slave trade, they shared common Bantu words. The Bantu language perhaps started in Nubia and spread throughout the Bantu speaking regions of Africa, and perhaps, is the basis for the ancient Egyptian language as well. See Appendices.

12

The African Renaissance

Perhaps it is easier to feel contempt toward a people who are deemed to be inferior or uncivilized. This is the reason that racists find it necessary to falsely malign and marginalize the historical achievement of Africans. To overcome such racism as well as internalized racism, a corrected historical perspective is imperative. A correct historical perspective, like a compass, guides us toward a renewal of culture and an African renaissance; thus, this book has addressed the following:

Who originated civilization? When did the concept of *race* and religion first appear in human history? What are the historical events that contributed to the ideology of racism? The anxieties and insecurities, which breed the extreme contempt of some whites, towards people of color?

As previously noted, the invention of the arts and sciences came into being after thousands of years of Africans living and adapting to their environment. It was not a cold and harsh environment, like Europe, from which one could only hope to escape. The Africans were endowed with the Nile Valley, by the Creator. What the African people created in return for the gift, was a blessing for all humanity.

In the Egyptian religion, wisdom was the highest virtue, and learning the arts and sciences was synonymous with spirituality. Because by learning the liberal arts and sciences, one could in turn, liberate the soul, thus the term *liberal arts* and the famous quote *the truth shall set you free*. Perhaps it should be our quest today, to equate learning with spirituality.

After the development of the arts and sciences, Egyptian priests and scribes incorporated them into a kind of spiritual ethic and philosophy called the Egyptian Mystery System. It was the religion and culture of African people, as George James describes in *Stolen Legacy*:

> ...Egypt was the holy land of the ancient world and the Mysteries were the one, ancient and holy Catholic religion, whose power was supreme. This lofty culture

system of the Black people filled Rome with envy, and consequently she legalized Christianity, which she had persecuted for five centuries, and set it up as a state religion and as a rival of Mysteries, its own mother. This is why the Mysteries have been despised; this is why other ancient religions of the Black people are despised; because they are all offspring of the African Mysteries, which have never been clearly understood by Europeans, and consequently have provoked their prejudice and condemnation.[1]

According historical evidence, the Egyptian Mystery System is the earliest theory of salvation in world history. The method for obtaining this salvation was to achieve a balance between learning the arts and sciences and living a virtuous life. The Mystery System included the following Seven Liberal Arts:

1. Grammar
2. Rhetoric
3. Logic
4. Geometry
5. Arithmetic
6. Astronomy
7. Music[2]

Since Africans invented these subjects, African children should approach the learning of those subjects with full confidence in their abilities to master them.

The Mystery system also included these Ten Virtues:

(1) Control of thought
(2) Control of action
Both combined are equivalent to Justice and the righteousness of thought and action.
(3) Steadfastness of purpose
Equivalent to Fortitude
(4) Identity with spiritual life or of higher ideals.
Equivalent to Temperance
(5) Evidence of having a mission in life
(6) Evidence of a call to spiritual Orders of the Priesthood in the Mysteries
Both are equivalent to Prudence or of deep insight
(7) Freedom from resentment (when under the experience of prosecution or wrong)
Equivalent to courage
(8) Confidence in the power of the master (Teacher)
(9) Confidence in one's own ability to learn
Both are equivalent to Fidelity
(10) Readiness or preparedness for initiation[3]

Why is African history important for children in particular? The confidence level of all children including children of African descent depends for the most part on either their own successes, or the successes of others who look like them. Some children, however, may not find successful role models immediately around them; therefore, they should learn African history in the home, at a very early age. Once aware of the African invention of mathematics, writing, grammar, science, etc., they will achieve far and above the low expectations of today's modern education system.

Ancestral Symbols for Wisdom

In addition to the Mystery System above, African symbols are extremely important in a cultural context because of the following:

> Once the symbol is formed, it is capable of acting upon the brain-computer, which receives it as an energy or data message. This message effect the end-product of behavior as carried forth in any area of human activity. The symbol, in turn, acts upon the external environment. These "single-picture-sentences" or "single–picture-paragraphs" commence in the brain-computer and act as powerful undetected persuaders, and thus, as powerful determinants of behavioral patterns.[4]

The quote above is from *Isis Papers*, by Dr. Welsing. In it, she also writes that, "Symbolism is thus the glue that holds the individual and collective psyche of the people and the culture together." Obviously then, while symbols hold the people and its culture together, they also give insight into the culture itself—the values, ethics, customs and traditions of the people.

Some symbols such as African Adinkra symbols, symbolize brotherhood, faith or charity; and serve as reminders of African culture, tradition and values. Adinkra symbols among other things can remind our children about proper behavior. This is a very important aspect of a strong cultural tradition; knowing what to do and how to behave in any given situation. The mish mash that is American culture can be quite confusing in this respect; because American culture is simply *do what you want* and that is no culture at all.

There is a concerted effort in America to prevent the teaching of white supremacy and racism. Critical Race Theory (CRT), which was conceived in law schools, based on the general idea of white supremacy and racism that oppresses and subjugates African descent people to the lower class of American society; and the crucial role of the American justice system. Donald Trump said CRT was anti-American and could not be used in any government diversity inclusion programs. This was red meat for conservatives who called CRT racist and divisive. Legislators in several states are now writing laws to ban the teachings of white supremacy and racism. So, in effect, CRT is being debated as if white supremacy and racism were theory. In fact, the title Critical Race Theory itself is a misnomer because there is nothing theoretical about white supremacy and racism. Although based upon the false concept of race, the ideology of racism itself is not speculation or supposition. It is not a theory but a real, active proven ideology based on the false notion of a white superiority over the false notion of the inferiority of people of African descent. In fact, Critical Race Theory should have been named Racism 101. Racism is inseparable from the teachings of African and African American history, and should be inseparable from the teachings of American history. Yet there is an effort to ban books such as this one in K-12 curriculum. In other words, CRT is a catchall phrase used by racists to ban the teaching of our African history.

Therefore, with books such as this one, we must teach our true African history at home starting from pre-kindergarten and impart to our children our cultural love of learning and education; and demand and expect from them nothing short of excellence. Also, the teaching of Maat principles can help reestablish culture in the community. We certainly cannot afford another lost generation believing that doing anything you want when you want is in fact culture.

African American children, because of their unique background, should study longer and focus harder than anyone else, and regain the passion for learning that is in our culture. Adults could refresh their skills in reading, writing, grammar, and mathematics, to pass along those skills to the children at home.

Adults and children could embrace Maat in general and these seven principles of Maat: Truth, Balance, Order, Harmony, Righteousness, Morality and Justice. Along with the negative confessions, which are a part of the overall values, ethics, and traditions of African people. Negative Confessions along with Maat principles and morals can shape and guide one's actions. This understanding, in combination with the understanding of the first two Virtues: *Control of thought*, and *Control of action*, will enable a restoration of a system of justice within the community. When you control your mind, you control your yourself; and when you control yourself, you gain a master. This practice of self-regulation in the community would require less need for hostile systems of external justice.

When African descent children come to know their history, and thus come to know themselves, they will gain a new found wisdom, confidence, discipline, self-respect, and respect toward one another. Our children possessing these attributes along with a renewed sense of unity will inevitably spark the new African renaissance.

THE END

APPENDICES

(A) Inventors

Louis Alexander
(Light Control, Burglar Alarm, Television Tubes)
Harrison Allen
(Ignition of Solid Propellant Rocket Motors)
Jeremiah Baltimore
(Stationary Steam Engine)
Charles Banks
(Jack – Sept 2, 1930, Release Valve- Jan 10, 1933, Hydraulic Jack- May 13, 1930)
A.J. Beard
(Railroad Car Coupler, Rotary Engine)
J.W. Benton
(Derrick for Hoisting)
Henry Blair
(Corn and Cotton Planting Devices, Corn Planter- Oct 14, 1834, Cotton Planter- Aug 31, 1836)
David Boker
(Inner Tube)
Henry Bowman
(Flags)
Otis Boykin
(Control Arm for Artificial Heart Stimulator, Electrical Device used on all Guided Missiles and

IBM Computers)
Hugh Brown
(Device to Govern Position of Dampers in a Furnace)
Maria Van Brittan Brown and Albert L. Brown
(Home Security System Utilizing Television Surveillance)
Solomon Brown
(Assisted Stanley Morse in Development of Telegraph Device)
Charles Bryant
(Auto Seat Bed)
George Caruthers
(Ultraviolet Spectrograph)
Oscar Cassel
(Flight Machine – 1925)
David N. Crosthwait, Jr.
(Heating Systems, Thermostats and Refrigeration)
Shelby J. Davidson
(Postal and other Office Equipment)
Joseph Hunter Dickinson
(Improved Musical Instruments and Player Pianos- 1889)
William Douglas
(Various Inventions for Harvesting)
James Doyle
(Automatic Serving System)
Wilbert Dyer
(Satellite Tracker)
Frank J. Ferrell
(Valves for Steam Engines, Steam Valves, Steam Trap- Feb 11, 1890)

James Forten
(Apparatus for Managing Sails, Sail Control-1850)
Meredith Gourdine
(Device to Convert Gas into High Voltage Electricity; Exhaust Purification Device for Automobiles; Air Pollution measuring Device, Generators for Power Stations)
Hale
(Automobile-1928)
Lloyd Augustus Hall
(Patented methods of Preserving and Sterilizing Foods)
Solomon Harper
(Blocking System for Controlling Railway Trains)
Tony Helm
(All Angle Wrench Attachment)
Andrew Hilyer
(Hot Air Register and Water Evaporator; Water Evaporator Attachment for Hot Air Register- Aug 26, 1890, Registers- Oct 14, 1890)
Benjamin F. Jackson
(Improved Heating and Lighting Device)
Jack Johnson
(Heavyweight champion, Wrench- Aug. 18, 1922)
Paul Johnson
(Therapeutic lamps)
Frederick McKinley Jones
(Air Conditioning for Truck and Railroad transportation of Food)
Clarence Larry
(Camera)

Lewis Howard Latimer
(Developed Carbon Arc Lights-improved Thomas Edison's Light Bulb)
W.A. Lavallette
(Printing Press- Sept 17, 1878)
Robert Benjamin Lewis
(Invented Machine to Improve Shipbuilding)
W.G. Madison
(Airship-1912)
Jan Ernst Matzeliger
(Shoe Lasting Device; Mechanism for Distributing Tacks- Nov 26, 1899; Nailing Machine- Feb 25, 1896; Tack Separating Mechanism-March 25, 1890; Lasting Machine-Sep 22, 1891)
Elijah McCoy
(Lubricating Cup for railroad Locomotives- July 2, 1872)
Emmanuel E. Moore
(Earth Moving machine)
George W. Murray
(Improved Agriculture Implements)
James Parson
(Austenite Alloy Steels)
Charles Patterson
(Vehicle Dash)
George Peake
(Hand Mill for Grinding Grain)
Robert A. Pelham
(Improved Office Equipment-Tabulator)
J.F. Pickering
(Airship-1900, Fountain Pen- Jan 7, 1890)

Charles V. Richey
(Improved Telephone Devices)
Norbert Rillieux
(Invented Multiple Effect Vacuum and Evaporator for Sugar Production-1846)
Elbert R. Robertson
(Chilled groove Wheel for Railroads)
Meloneze Robinson
(Surgical Support)
Adolphus Samms
(Airframe Center support Designed to Eliminate Second and Third Stage Engines in Multi-Stage Rockets)
Orvilee Slaughter
(Distress Radio)
Brinay Smart
(Valve Gears)
Richard B. Spikes
(Railroad Semaphore Automatic Directional Signals and Automatic Transmission Devices; Combination Milk Bottle Opener and Bottle Cover –June 29, 1926; Method and apparatus for Obtaining Average Samples and temperature of Tank Liquids – Oct 27, 1931; Automatic Gear Shift – Dec 6, 1932; Self-Locking Rack for Billiard Cues – 1910; Automatic shoe Shine Chair – 1939; Multiple Barrel Machine Gun – 1940)
John Standard
(Oil Stove – Oct 29, 1889; Refrigerator – July 14, 1891)
Rufus Stokes
(Air Purification Devices)

Clifton Sudbury
(Hydraulic Simulator)
Lewis Temple
(Invented Whaling Harpoon)
Norval Cobb Vaughn
(Bullet Proof Shield)
Madame C.J. Walker
(Cosmetic and Hair Products)
Andrew D. Washington
(Shoe Horn)
H.C. Webb
(Machine for Removing Palmettos)
Clarence White
(Network Impedance Calculator, Two Dimensional Slide Rule)
J.E. Whooter
(Airship-1914)
A.P. Ashbourne
(Biscuit Cutter-Nov 30, 1985)
L.C. Bailey
(Folding Bed- July 5, 1899)
G.E. Becket
(Letter Box- Oct 4, 1892)
L. Bell
(Locomotive Smoke Stack- May 23, 1871)
M.E. Benjamin
(Gong and Signal Chairs for Hotels- July 17, 1888)
M.W. Binga
(Street Sprinkling Apparatus- July 22, 1879)
A.B. Blackburn
(Railway Signal- Jan 10, 1888)

Sarah Boone
(Ironing Board- April 26, 1892)
Charles B. Brooks
(Punch- Oct 31, 1893; Street-Sweeper- march 17, 1896; Street Sweeper- April 21, 1896; Dust-Proof bag for street Sweepers- May 12, 1896)
Oscar E. Brown
(Horseshoe- Aug 23, 1892)
J.A. Burr
(Lawn Mower- May 9, 1899)
J.W. Butts
(Luggage Carrier- Oct 10, 1899)
W.C. Carter
(Umbrella Stand- Aug 4, 1885)
T.S. Church
(Carpet Beating Machine- July 29, 1884)
G. Cook
(Automatic Fishing Device- May 10, 1899)
J. Cooper
(Elevator Device- April 2, 1895)
P.W. Cornwell
(Draft Regulator- Feb 7, 1893)
A.L. Cralle
(Ice Cream Mold- Feb 2, 1897)
W.R. Davis, Jr.
(Library Table- Sep 24, 1878)
C.J. Dorticus
(Machine for Embossing Photos- April 16, 1895)
Clarence L. Elder
(Bidirectional Monitoring and Control System- 'Occustat' – Dec 28, 1976)

T. Elkins
(Refrigerating Apparatus- Nov 4, 1879)
F. Fleming, Jr.
(Guitar Variation- March 3, 1886)
G.F. Grant
(Golf Tee- Dec12, 1899)
J. Gregory
(Motor- April 26, 1887)
M. Headen
(Foot Power Hammer- Oct 5, 1886)
Garrett A. Morgan
(Gas Mask- Oct 13, 1914; Breathing Device- March 24, 1914; Traffic Signal- Nov 20, 1923)
B.F. Jackson
(Gas Burner- April 4, 1899)
William B. Purvis
(Invented Procedures for Making Paper Bags- Aug 12, 1890; Fountain Pen- Jan 7, 1890)
B. F Jackson
(Gas Burner- April 4, 1899)
Fredrick M. Jones
(Automatic refrigeration System)
J.L. Love
(Pencil Sharpener- 1897)

H. Spears
(Portable Shield for Infantry- Dec 27, 1870)
E. H. Sutton
(Cotton Cultivator- April 7, 1878)
Granville T. Woods
(Electromechanical Brake- Aug 16, 1887; Railway

Telegraphy- Nov 15, 1887; Induction Telegraph System- Nov 29, 1887; Overhead Conducting System for Electric Railway- May 29, 1888; Electromotive Railway System for long-haul Trucks- June 26, 1888)
Thomas L. Jennings
(Invented a Method for Dry Cleaning of Clothes- March 3, 1821)[5]

(B) *Adinkra Symbols*

Gye Nyame-Symbol of the omnipotence and immortality of God.

Fofoo-Symbol of jealousy, envy.

Akoma Ntoaso-Symbol of agreement or charter.

Ohene Niwa-The King has lots of eyes,
nothing is hidden from him.

Bi-nka-bi Obi nka obi- Unity.
Bite not one another, avoid conflict.

Nsoroma-Symbol of the child of the heavens.
I do not depend on myself.

Odenkyem-A crocodile lives in water yet breaths air not water.

Afena-Symbol of the ceremonial sword

Funtunfunafu-Need for unity, especially when there is one destiny.

Sepow-Symbol of law and justice.

Ako-ben-A war horn, call to battle.

Eban-Symbol of safety, security and love.

Vass, *The Bantu Speaking Heritage of the United States*, 43-60)

(C) *Bantu in America*

Place Names	Bantu Names
Alabama	Bantu
Ambato	Ambata
Cheaha	Tsiahu
Chelopa	Tshitupa
Chewacla	Tshiwaakula
Cotopa	Kuatupa
Congo	Kongo
Cotaco	Kotaku
Chipola	Tsipola
Chilota	Tsilota
Chuchula	Tshutshulua
Georgia	Bantu
Cataula	Katuulua
Chennba	Tshiema
Choestoe	Tshiotu
Chula	Tchula
Echota	A tshiota
Fulemmy	Fulama
Halloca	Haluka
Inaha	Hinaha
Suwanee	Nsub' wanyi
Picola	Mpikula

Florida	Bantu
Alfalfa	Alue papa
Chacala	Tshia kale
Chuluota	Tshilota
Chumukla	Tshiumukila
Kanapaha	Kena papa
Kolokee	Kuoloki
Suwanee	(n) Sub-wanyi
Tomoka	Tumuka
Tuscawilla	Tusawila
Uceta	Usheta

Mississippi	Bantu
Bobo	Bobo
Bolatusha	Baluatshisha
Hushpukena	Hushamukana
Kolola Springs	Kolola
Lula	Lula
Osyka	Oshika
Shongalo	Jonguela
Tchula	Tchula
Yockanookany	Yaku, nukana
Zama	Zama

North Carolina	Bantu
Aketiyi	A kuetu
Angola	Angola
Buquo	Buko
Cashie River	Kashia
Gela	Ngela
Cheoah	Tshiowa
Makatoka	Mua Katoka
Quaqua	Kuakua
Solola	Solola
Wakulla	Wakula

South Carolina	Bantu
Alcolu	Alkana
Becca	Beka
Beetaw	Bita
Boyano	Mbuy' enu
Boo-Boo	Mbubu
Booshopee	Bushipi
Calwasie	Kaluatshi
Chachan	Tshiatshiakana
Chinch Row	Tshinji
Cooterborougha	Nkuda

South Carolina	Bantu
Cuakles	Kuakulas
Dongola	Ndongola
Eady town	Idi
Gippy	Tshipi
Hoot gap	Huta
Opopome	Apopome
Palawana	Palua wanyi
Peedee	Mpidi
Pooshee	Mpuishi
Quocaratchie	Kuokolatshi

South Carolina	Bantu
Toogoodoo	Tukuta
Tullifinny	Tula mfinu
Untsaiyi	Utusadila
Wadboo	Wa ndapu
Wantoot	Wa ntutu
Wappaoolah	Wapaula
Watacoo	Wataku
Wimbee	Muimbi
Wosa	Wosa
Yoa	Yowa

Virginia	Bantu
Acca	Aka!
Arcola	Akula
Bena	Bena
Cash	Kasha
Chula	Tchula
Dongola	Ndongola
Ino	Inanyi
Ka	Ka!
Lanexa	Langesha
Leck	Leka

Virginia	Bantu
Mobjack	Mombejaku
Nandua	Nendue
Nominye	Numanye
Onemo	Unema
Tola	Ntola
Wakema	Wakunuua
Wakenva	Wakema
Zacata	Zakata
Zanoni	(mu) Sononyi
Zuni	(mu) Sunyi

NOTES

Chapter 1
[1] Rick Weiss, "Scientists Find A DNA Change That Accounts For White Skin" *Washington Post,* December 16, 2005

Chapter 2
[1] Ahmed Osman, *Moses And Akhenaten*, Rochester Vermont, Bear & Company, 1990, pp 61-67

Chapter 3

Chapter 4
[1] Osman, *Moses and Akhenaten*, p 160
[2] Ahmed Osman, *Jesus in the House of the Pharaohs*, Rochester Vermont, Bear & Company, 1992, pp 185-186
[3] *Ibid.*, p 188
[4] *Ibid.*, pp 69-70
[5] Osman, Moses and Akhenaten, p 29
[6] Robert Bauval, Thomas Brophy, Ph.D., *Black Genesis*, Rochester Vermont, Bear & Company, 2011, p 102
[7] *Ibid.*, p 242
[8] *Ibid.*, p 94
[9] Cheikh Anta Diop, *The African Origin of Civilization*, Chicago, Lawrence Hill & Co., 1974, p 91
[10] Bauval, Brophy, *Black Genesis*, p 119
[11] Osman, *Moses and Akhenaten*, pp 28-29
[12] Flavius Josephus, *Josephus The complete Works*, translated by William Whiston, Nashville Tennessee, Thomas Nelson Publishers, 1998, p 114
[13] Diop *The African Origin of Civilization*, p 138

Chapter 5
[1] Josephus, *Josephus The complete Works*, p 926
[2] *Ibid.*, p 932
[3] Osman, *Moses and Akhenaten*, p 28
[4] Josephus, *The Complete Works*, p 943
[5] *Ibid.*, p 945
[6] E.A. Wallace Budge, *The Egyptian Book of the Dead*, New York, Dover Publications, Inc, 1967, pp 347-349

[7] *Ibid.*, p 44
[8] *Ibid.*, p 576
[9] Henry Louis Gates Jr., *Wonders of the African World*, New York, Alfred A. Knopf, 1999, p 20
[10] Chester G. Starr, *The Roman Empire*, New York, Oxford University Press, 1982, p 3
[11] *Ibid.*
[12] Herodotus, *Histories Book 2*, pp 137-138

Chapter 6
[1] Arthur Koestler, *The Thirteenth Tribe*, New York, Random House, 1976, pp 1-2
[2] *Ibid.*, p 15
[3] *Ibid.*, pp 15-16
[4] *Ibid.*, p 160
[5] *Ibid.*, p 17

Chapter 7
[1] George G. M. James, Stolen Legacy, New York, Philosophical Library, 1954, p 1
[2] *Ibid.*, pp 5-6
[3] *Ibid.*, p 7
[4] *Ibid.*
[5] *Ibid.*, pp 30-31
[6] *Ibid.*, p 31
[7] Herodotus, *Histories Book 2*, p 139
[8] *Ibid*, p 143
[9] *Ibid.*
[10] *Ibid.*

Chapter 8
[1] Herodotus, *Histories Book 2*, p 151
[2] *Ibid.*, p 154
[3] Diop, *The African Origin of Civilization*, pp 158-159
[4] Mark Hyman, *Blacks Before America*, Trenton, New World Press, 1994, p 21
[5] James Henry Breasted, *The Edwin Smith Surgical Papyrus*, The University of Chicago Press, 1930, p 10
[6] *Ibid.*

[7] *Ibid.*, p 12
[8] *Ibid.*, p 13
[9] *Ibid.*, p 16
[10] *Ibid.*, pp 78-425
[11] A. B. Chase, H.P. Manning, *The Rhind Mathematical Papyrus British Museum 10057 and 10058*, Oberlin, Ohio, Mathematical association of America, 1927-29
[12] *Ibid.*
[13] *Ibid.*
[14] *Ibid.*
[15] *Ibid.*
[16] Diop, *The African Origin of Civilization*, p 233
[17] Robert Steven Bianchi, *Daily Life of the Nubians*, Connecticut, Greenwood Press, 2004, pp 216-217
[18] Diop, *The African Origin of Civilization*, pp 147-148

Chapter 9
[1] Diop, *The African Origin of Civilization*, p 110
[2] Poe, *Black Spark White Fire*, p 6
[3] *Ibid.*, p 14
[4] *Ibid.*, p 6
[5] Diop, *The African Origin of Civilization*, pp 111-113
[6] Mark Hyman, *Blacks Before America*, Trenton, New World Press, 1994, p 3
[7] *Ibid.*, p 4
[8] *Ibid.*, p 130

Chapter 10
[1] Basil Davidson, *The African Slave Trade*, Boston/Toronto, Little, Brown and company, 1980, p 13
[2] *Ibid.*, p 14
[3] Paul Bohannan, Philip Curtin, *Africa and Africans*, New York, The Natural History Press, 1971, p 45
[4] *Ibid.*, p 46
[5] *Ibid.*, p 51
[6] James Ridgeway, *Blood in the Face*, New York, Thunder's Mouth Press,1990, p 186)
[7] David M. Chalmers, *Hooded Americanism*, Durham, Duke University Press,1987, p 412

[8] *Ibid.*, p 429
[9] *Ibid.*, p 424
[10] www.sciencemag.org/content/328/5979/710.full
[11] Ridgeway, *Blood in the Face*, p 148
[12] *Ibid.*, p 90

Chapter 11
[1] Basil Davidson, *African Kingdoms*, Virginia, Time-Life Books, 1966, pp 168-169
[1] Diop, *The African Origin of Civilization*, p 140
[2] *Ibid.*, p 198
[3] Winifred Kellersberger Vass, *The Bantu Speaking Heritage of the United States*, Los Angeles, CAAS, 1979, PP 25-26
[4] *Ibid.*, p 27
[5] *Ibid.*, p 3
[6] *Ibid.*, p 29

Chapter 12
[1] George G. M. James, Stolen Legacy, pp 154-155
[2] *Ibid.*, 28
[3] *Ibid.*, 30
[4] Dr. Frances Cress Welsing, *The Isis Papers*, Chicago, Third World Press, 1991, p 55
Appendices
[5] www.princeton.edu/-mcbrown/display/inventor list.htm

BIBLIOGRAPHY

Agnese, George, Re, Maurizio, *Ancient Egypt*. New York: Barnes and Noble, Inc., 2006

Asante, Molefi Kete, *The History of Africa*. New York: Routledge, Taylor and Franis Group, 2007

Bauval, Robert, Brophy, Ph.D., Thomas, *Black Genesis*. Rochester, Vermont: Bear & Company, 2011

Bianchi, Robert Steven, *Daily Life of the Nubians*. Connecticut: Greenwood Press, 2004

Bohannan, Paul, Curtin, Philip, *Africa and Africans*. New York: The Natural History Press, 1971

Breasted, James Henry, *The Edwin Smith Surgical Papyrus*. Chicago: The University of Chicago Press, 1930

Budge, E.A. Wallace, *The Egyptian Book of the Dead*. New York: Dover Publications, Inc, 1967

Chalmers, David M., *Hooded Americanism*. Durham: Duke University Press, 1987

Chase, A. B., Manning, H.P., *The Rhind Mathematical Papyrus British Museum 10057 and 10058*. Ohio: Mathematical Association of America, 1927-29

Davidson, Basil, *African Kingdoms*. Virginia: Time-Life Books, 1966

___. *The African Slave Trade*. Boston: Little, Brown & Company, 1980

Diop, Cheikh Anta, *The African Origin of Civilization*. Chicago: Lawrence Hill & Co., 1974

Gates Jr., Henry Louis, *Wonders of the African World*. New York: Alfred A. Knopf, 1999

Herodotus, *Histories* Book 2. C 430BC

Hyman, Mark, *Blacks Before America*. Trenton, NJ: Africa World Press, Inc., 1994

James, George G. M., *Stolen Legacy*. New York:

Philosophical Library, 1954

Josephus, Flavius, Whiston, William, translator, *Josephus The complete Works.*
Nashville: Thomas Nelson Publishers, 1998

Koestler, Arthur, *The Thirteenth Tribe.* New York: Random House, 1976

Neugebauer, O., Parker, Richard A., *Egyptian Astrological Texts.* Rhode Island: Brown University Press, 1964

Osman, Ahmed, *Moses and Akhenaten.* Rochester, Vermont: Bear & Company, 1990

___. *Jesus in the House of the Pharaohs.* Rochester, Vermont: Bear & Company, 1992

Ridgeway, James, *Blood in the Face.* New York: Thunder's Mouth Press, 1990

Shirer, William L., *The Rise and Fall of the Third Reich.* New York: Simon and Schuster, 1960

Schock, Ph.D., Robert M., McNally, Robert Aquinas, *Voyage of the Pyramid Builders.* New York: Penguin Group, 2003

Starr, Chester G., *The Roman Empire.* New York: Oxford University Press, 1982

Vass, Winifred Kellersberger, *The Bantu Speaking Heritage of the United States.* UCLA: 1979

Welsing, Frances Cress, *The Isis Papers.* Chicago: Third World Press, 1991

www.ingramcontent.com/pod-product-compliance
Lightning Source LLC
Chambersburg PA
CBHW031143160426
43193CB00008B/240